IT HAPPENED IN

THE GREAT SMOKIES

IT HAPPENED IN

THE GREAT SMOKIES

Stories of Events and People that
SHAPED A NATIONAL PARK

Second Edition

MICHAEL R. BRADLEY

Globe
Pequot GUILFORD, CONNECTICUT

Globe
Pequot

An imprint of The Rowman & Littlefield Publishing Group, Inc.
4501 Forbes Blvd., Ste. 200
Lanham, MD 20706
www.rowman.com

Distributed by NATIONAL BOOK NETWORK

Copyright © 2020 The Rowman and Littlefield Publishing Company, Inc.

Map by The Rowman and Littlefield Publishing Company, Inc.

British Library Cataloguing in Publication Information available

Library of Congress Cataloging-in-Publication Data available

ISBN 978-1-4930-3974-6 (paperback)
ISBN 978-1-4930-3975-3 (e-book)

∞™ The paper used in this publication meets the minimum requirements of American National Standard for Information Sciences—Permanence of Paper for Printed Library Materials, ANSI/NISO Z39.48-1992.

CONTENTS

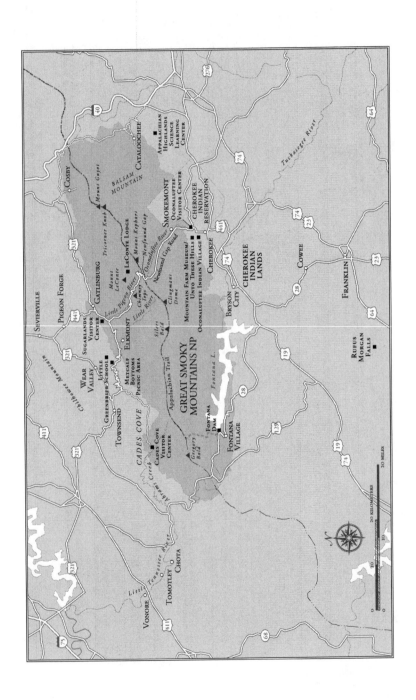

PREFACE

There is a place in the southeastern United States, where North Carolina and Tennessee share a common border, that is magical. At that place, mountain peaks stretch steeply upward, their heights shrouded in an almost constant smoky haze. Clear streams tumble over boulders as they rush downhill. A myriad of trees shade the ground while numberless wildflowers lift their blossoms above the forest floor.

People have lived among these mountains since the dawn of history, and they have all learned to love these hills. From the unknown earliest Native Americans to the Cherokee to the pioneer settlers to the men and women of today, these hills have spoken a message of peace, beauty, and relaxation.

This magical place is the Great Smoky Mountains. At present, millions of people visit the national park, which protects much of the area, preserving the hills for the future. Most of the park visitors see its beauty through the windows of their cars, whereas a few don boots and knapsacks to huff and puff their way over the rolling trails. Whether seen sitting in a car or while hiking a rugged path, the mountains reveal themselves, both in macro- and microscopic ways to visitors who look carefully.

These mountains are the oldest mountains in North America. The Great Smoky Mountains National Park offers both easy road access and challenging hikes and pleasant strolls through its ancient natural wonders. But the story of the park is more than the eons-long record of nature at work. The human residents of the area have left their mark on the land and have created a unique culture in this unique place.

This book reveals some of the stories of these residents and of their culture. Some of these residents lived long ago, and some are contemporary, but through their stories you can get a glimpse of their love for the Great Smoky Mountains, a love you are encouraged to come and share.

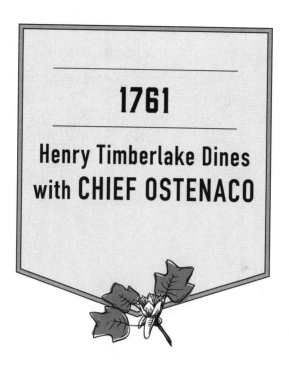

1761

Henry Timberlake Dines
with CHIEF OSTENACO

Relations between the white settlers and the Cherokee fluctuated as they were affected by larger historical forces. From 1754 to 1761 relations were poor as the Cherokee took the side of the French in the Seven Years' War. The end of that war brought the Cherokee into a friendly relationship with the British authorities and the settlers, because the British agreed to stop the westward expansion of settlement.

During this peaceful interlude, Lieutenant Henry Timberlake of Virginia was assigned to explore the Overhill country and to produce a map of the area. (The map he created was so accurate that it is still used by present-day archaeologists.) The Overhill Cherokee, so named because they lived west of the mountains in what is now the area of Great Smoky Mountains National Park, invited Timberlake to visit as they were anxious to prove their loyalty to the British following the defeat of the French. Because the traditional Cherokee way of life had not yet been altered by the too-frequent contact with European ways, Timberlake would see the best of Cherokee life and culture, which culminated in a memorable visit with Ostenaco, chief of Tomotley town.

Timberlake began his journey at the Long Island of the Holston River, located in present-day Kingsport, Tennessee. For twenty-two days he floated and paddled down the Holston to its juncture with the Tennessee River, then down the Tennessee to the Little Tennessee, and then up that stream to the Overhill towns.

These towns impressed Timberlake. Each consisted of a cluster of houses spread out over several acres with each family choosing its own site to build their home. The houses were constructed of small poles set in the ground in a circle. Bamboo canes were woven into the poles so that the framework resembled an upside-down basket. Then mud was plastered over the framework to a thickness of a foot or more. The house was then topped with a thatched roof. Each town also had its meetinghouse and a "square ground," where dances and religious ceremonies were held.

At Chota, one of the Cherokee towns, Timberlake visited a meeting hall, or townhouse, built of timber and covered with earth so that it looked to him like a small mountain shaped like a sugar loaf. Inside, rows of seats were positioned in tiers around the walls, with a separate section for each of the seven clans found in every Cherokee town. The clans were called Wolf, Deer, Bird, Paint, Blue, Long Hair, and Kituwah. The meetinghouse could hold about five hundred people. Timberlake found that when an assembly was held in the meeting hall, women had a respected voice in decision making and that they spoke freely in the assemblies.

At Tomotley, Timberlake received his warmest welcome, an event that he remembered the rest of his life. A short distance outside the town, Timberlake was met by Chief Ostenaco, who was about sixty years old, his brothers and sisters, and his mother.

As Ostenaco and his family led Timberlake into the town, a crowd of about four hundred Cherokee assembled. In front of the crowd were a dozen young men, naked except for loincloths, with their bodies painted in curious designs. The young men led the whole party into the town, waving fans made of eagle feathers and dancing in intricate steps. The rest of the townspeople were dressed in traditional Cherokee clothing. The men wore brightly colored cloth, headbands, wrapped in turban fashion. Many men wore knee-length, loose-fitting shirts of bright cloth; others wrapped their upper bodies in blankets. Cloth or buckskin trousers were the rule. Women wore dresses, many made of cloth obtained by trading; young children wore shirts only.

The whole town followed Ostenaco, Timberlake, and the dancers into the townhouse, where a fire burned in the middle of the floor. The head men and women of the town sat nearest to the fire, along with Timberlake; the others all took seats around them.

More species of tree are found in the Great Smoky Mountains National Park than are found in the entire continent of Europe.

Several of the Cherokee made speeches. Timberlake's command of the Cherokee language was imperfect, but he understood that the intent of the speeches was to welcome him to their town. After the speeches, a pipe was passed around the circle nearest the fire. Timberlake, a little squeamish about this custom, later wrote, "I put on the best face I was able, although I dared not even wipe the end of the pipe that came out of their mouths."

Then it was time to eat, and everyone moved outside. Timberlake and some of the town leaders sat under a thatched-roof shelter, but most of the townspeople sat wherever they felt like sitting. There were no eating utensils other than the knives that most everyone carried on their belts, so hands were freely used as both plates and spoons.

Several kinds of meat were offered: venison, bear, buffalo, and a variety of small game. Timberlake was not impressed with the taste of the meat, finding it overcooked and lacking in all spices. This, of course, was the result of the traditional Cherokee way of roasting meat over an open fire. They had no spices with which to flavor food except salt.

There was also a grand selection of vegetables, for the Cherokee obtained most of their food by farming, supplementing their food by hunting and gathering. Many of the crops grown by the Cherokee are now considered staples worldwide, although they were unknown in Europe until the discovery of the New World. Thus, Timberlake was offered pumpkins, squash, butter beans, peas, both white and sweet potatoes, boiled corn on the cob, and hominy. The potatoes were roasted in the ashes of a cooking fire, and the other vegetables were all boiled or simmered.

Trade had brought some iron kettles to Tomotley, but much of the cooking was still done in clay bowls into which hot rocks had been placed. The cooked vegetables were then passed around in gourds. Two of Timberlake's favorites from the feast were corn bread and a drink made of hominy, which had been pounded into a mush, mixed with water, and simmered over a slow fire.

People ate until they had all they wanted. Some wandered to their homes; others stayed for drumming and dancing. Drummers played three kinds of drums, each sounding a different note, and dancers carried rattles made of dried gourds that contained small pieces of gravel. The lead woman dancer had special rattles made of turtle shells, which were strapped to each leg. As some dancers got tired and drifted away to go to sleep, others came back from their houses where they had been napping. The celebration continued until midnight, when a weary Timberlake found his way to his blankets.

The friendship that began that night between Timberlake and Ostenaco endured for many years. In time, Timberlake took his Cherokee friend to London, where Sir Joshua Reynolds painted his portrait and he was presented to the king. As an older man, Timberlake wrote that he longed to retire to the "hospitable country" of the Cherokee.

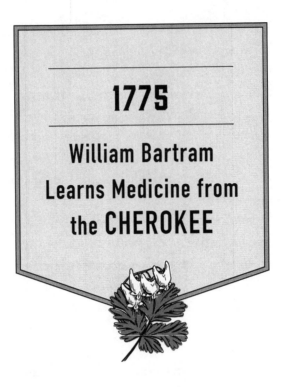

1775

William Bartram Learns Medicine from the CHEROKEE

William Bartram, one of the most famous naturalists ever born in America, was the son of a noted naturalist, John Bartram of Philadelphia. Until he was well into his adult years, William tried a variety of occupations, none successfully. At the age of thirty-five, he decided to give in to his natural inclination and follow in his father's footsteps and become a student of nature. His decision was strongly reinforced when Dr. John Fothergill, a leading physician of London, England, commissioned him to travel throughout the southern colonies in North America to collect plants, seeds, and vegetation to be sent to London. All medicines were herbal at that time, and Dr. Fothergill was hoping Bartram would discover new cures for old diseases.

Bartram spent four years exploring the South, traveling as far as the Spanish Territory of Florida. On his way back north, he met John Stuart of Charleston, South Carolina. Stuart, the royal government's agent to the Cherokee, told Bartram about the great variety of flora to be found in the Cherokee Overhill country, which included the Great Smoky Mountains. Bartram could not resist making the trip.

This was a dangerous time to travel in Cherokee country, however. War between the colonies and the home country was imminent, and the Cherokee had a history of siding with Britain in an attempt to hold back the tide of settlers. Since 1763 the British government had endeavored to keep the settlers east of the crest of the Appalachians, but without success. Unknown to Bartram, war would break out between the colonies and Britain before he even began his journey. Because of the danger, Bartram could find no one to guide him. A Quaker, he was committed to living in peace with all men. Confident that he could live peacefully with the Cherokee, he returned into their country alone. Among them, he found kindred spirits; they would become well known for their willingness to accept people of other races into their midst.

Bartram began his journey at the site of the old Cherokee town of Keowee in present-day South Carolina. He left in May, not knowing that the first shots of the American Revolution had been fired almost a month earlier. Travel was slow. Crossing rivers usually meant that all his belongings would be soaked, so he had to stop and dry out his things before moving on. Without corn to feed his horse, he had to spend some time each day letting the animal graze.

After several days of travel, Bartram could see the mountains looming on the horizon before him, and once he finally arrived, he was thrilled. He recorded in his journal that the mountains were "like Eden, a veritable Paradise."

In the mountains Bartram found a botanical treasure trove. There were more species of plants in this area than were on the entire continent of Europe and more plant diversity than in all the rest of North America. Instead of traveling hundreds of miles from the subtropics to Canada to study different types of plants, Bartram needed only to hike a few miles up the steep mountains to move from a subtropical to an alpine climate. He observed one Canadian species of bird, the junco, which never breed at high elevations. These Canadian juncos spent the summer at the top of the mountains and the winter at the bottom.

> *The Great Smoky Mountains National Park is the most visited of all national parks, receiving more than nine million visitors each year.*

Despite being a Quaker, Bartram held some beliefs that were pantheistic. He felt that there was a soul in all living things—plants and animals included. This struck a sympathetic chord with the Cherokee inhabitants of the mountains, who held a similar point of view concerning the world around them.

Although he did not know the Cherokee language, Bartram related well to them. On his way to Cowee one day, he stopped and sat on a log for a lunch of ship's biscuit, cheese, and water. A young Cherokee man came down the trail and did not see Bartram initially. When the naturalist spoke, the young man was startled, but soon the two were smiling and gesturing at one another. Before parting, Bartram said he "gave the young man a passel of good tobacco," and they were friends.

To learn from the Cherokee about the uses of the plants that grew in the mountains, Bartram needed an interpreter. At the town of Cowee, he found one, an Irishman named Galahan who had married a Cherokee woman. Galahan made a living trading with surrounding Cherokee towns and knew the country and its people well.

Bartram wanted to explore the countryside, but Galahan told him the situation was not suitable for white men to be wandering far afield into the Cherokee territory. Instead, Galahan introduced Bartram to the shaman, or medicine man, of Cowee.

The shaman was both a physician and a spiritual advisor to the community. He used a combination of herbal medicine and traditional religious practices, such as chants and dances, to cure illness. He also led religious ceremonies in an attempt to influence the outcome of important events such as hunting parties or military expeditions. With his wide knowledge of the area's plants, the shaman would be a valuable teacher to Bartram.

The Cherokee were convinced that for every disease there was a plant that provided a cure. Bartram witnessed the Cherokee using numerous plant remedies to relieve a variety of problems. By following the shaman into the woods and helping him collect plants, Bartram learned many of the traditional Cherokee uses of herbs.

One secret he did not fathom, however, was the preparation of the sacred "black drink." Before going to war, there would be a solemn ceremony in which the shaman collected leaves and twigs from a holly tree, mixed them with other ingredients, and made a dark-colored beverage that would be drunk with close observation of ritual by all those going to war. Bartram never discovered what physical effect the drink produced.

Almost all the medicinal uses of plants involved simmering parts of the plants in water to make a tea for drinking or pulverizing the plant to make a paste that was mixed with hot water to make a poultice, or thick paste, which was then spread on the afflicted body part. The list of Cherokee illnesses and their cures that Bartram learned include the following:

TO CURE	TAKE
Headache	Tea made from willow leaves
Diarrhea	Tea made from the inner bark of black oak trees
Hives	Catnip tea
Asthma	Place a poultice of sourwood bark on the chest.
Blisters	Place a poultice of wild cherry leaves on the blister.
Colds	Boneset tea
Fevers of all kinds	Feverweed tea
Intestinal parasites	Chew pinkroot.
"Tired blood"	Chew bloodroot.
Phlegm	Smoke the leaves of life-everlasting.
Pneumonia	Place a poultice of snakeroot on the chest.
Bladder infections	Drink tea made from ground ivy.
Infected wounds	Use a poultice made of catnip and beadwood bark.

Colic	Tea made from Sampson's snakeroot
Rheumatism	Dog-fennel tea
Bee stings	Cover the sting with a poultice of wet tobacco.

Bartram roamed the slopes close to Cowee, reflecting on this herbal knowledge for several weeks, and gathered specimens to take with him for further study. At last, the isolation of his location and the loneliness of having no one to talk with in English became depressing, and so he made his way to the coast and then home to Philadelphia.

Over the years since Bartram's stay in Cowee, modern science has come to respect many of the Cherokee ideas as containing the basis on which contemporary knowledge and technology can create effective medicines. We have Bartram to thank for helping to preserve the traditional medical knowledge of the Cherokee.

REVEREND ROBERT BUSHYHEAD

[1914–2001]

The survival of the Kituwah dialect of the Cherokee language owes much to the efforts of Reverend Robert Bushyhead. His history contains many recurring themes in the story of the Eastern Band of the Cherokee Nation. Just before the American Revolution the British government sent Captain James Stuart as an agent to the Cherokee Nation. Stuart had a thick growth of red hair and the Cherokee gave him the name of "Bushyhead." Stuart married into the Cherokee and his descendants became known as Bushyhead.

Stuart's son Robert was born in a one-room log house in the Birdtown community of the Qualla Boundary Indian Reservation on the southern edge of what is now the Great Smoky Mountains National Park. Robert spoke only Kituwah, until he was forced to attend a government school where only English was permitted. Robert graduated from that school and enrolled at Carson Newman College, a Baptist school, not far from his mountain home.

Robert returned to his original home as a minister. For many seasons he was one of the actors in the outdoor drama *Unto These Hills*, which tells the history of the Cherokee people. Not until the 1960s did he realize that the looming extinction of the Kituwah dialect meant the loss of much of the culture of the Cherokee people. He began collecting every written document he could find in Kituwah and worked with his schoolteacher daughter, Jean Blanton, to make recordings.

Reverend Bushyhead's efforts inspired the leadership of the Eastern Band of the Cherokee to begin a program to revitalize the Kituwah dialect. Today the language is taught to preschool classes as well as to older students. Reverend Bushyhead once noted that "No other language sounds exactly like Kituwah, and we want to preserve this."

His wish is today being realized.

1776

Nanye-hi Shames
THE WARRIORS

Nanye-hi was disgusted with the men of her tribe. War had begun between the American colonists and Great Britain more than a year earlier. The Cherokee knew the colonists were insatiable in their desire for land and, therefore, had no wish to see these people set up their own government. From the Cherokee perspective, the British government offered the best hope for the future. Since 1763 the British had been trying to hold back the flood of settlers by restricting new forts to the eastern slopes of the Appalachian Mountains. With this record in mind, the Cherokee were sympathetic to a message from John Stuart, the Royal Superintendent of Indian Affairs in South Carolina, asking the Cherokee to help in the war against the American colonists.

A great meeting was held in the council house at Chota, the most important of the Cherokee towns at that time and located on the Little Tennessee River, just west of the current National Park. At the meeting Stuart—who was visiting Shawnee leaders, such as Cornstalk—had urged joining the British in the war. Dragging Canoe, the most aggressive of the Cherokee leaders, and Osioota of Chilhowee urged their people to ally with the Shawnee and British forces. The older chiefs and Nanye-hi opposed the move, but they had been outvoted. The Cherokee had gone to war with the American settlers, and Nanye-hi was not happy.

Nanye-hi had the right to speak in the council as an equal of any of the male leaders, because she held the title of "Beloved Woman," or Ghighau, a position of great influence. She had been awarded this title around 1755. In that year the Cherokee were fighting their traditional enemies, the Creeks. In a battle at Taliwa, in modern-day north Georgia, Nanye-hi had been loading guns for her husband, Kingfisher, when he was mortally wounded. Nanye-hi took up the weapons of her fallen husband and fought as well as any man. When the victorious Cherokee returned to Chota, the tale of her bravery soon spread to all the towns of the tribe. In response to her bravery, she was made Ghighau for life.

Following the decision for war in the council house at Chota, Nanye-hi made a decision of her own. She was convinced that war would lead to disaster and that the only hope for the Cherokee was to live in peace with the settlers. She spoke to several white traders who were leaving the Cherokee towns, confirming the rumors they had heard that a decision had been made for war. Nanye-hi asked that these men spread a warning about the war through the white settlements, especially those in the Watauga area. This was done.

In July 1776 Dragging Canoe attacked white settlers at Island Flats, the present site of Kingsport, Tennessee, and was defeated. An attack on Watauga Fort by Old Abram, a leading Cherokee chief, met with a stalemate because the settlers were well prepared and had plenty of food and water in their stockade. The only positive result of these attacks for the Cherokee was the taking of two prisoners, Samuel Moore and Sarah Bean.

The returning Cherokee warriors were in an ugly mood. Their hopes for victory had met with disappointment. Men had been killed and wounded without anything gained, and a war had been started, which might lead to disaster for the tribe. Given this attitude, the future of the captives looked bleak. Samuel Moore was taken away to Tuskeegee town and was never seen again. Sarah Bean was brought to Toqua, a town near Nanye-hi's home at Chota.

At her home Nanye-hi heard that Sarah Bean was to be burned alive at Toqua, which was the reason for her disgust with the men of the tribe. She thought they were better people than that. It was true that tradition allowed for the death of a captive on occasion, but the death was not supposed to be a matter of vengeance, much less an execution brought on by frustration and anger.

Nanye-hi was no stranger to the violent realities of life in her time and place. She had won her position as Ghighau in battle. But her people were not violent by nature and, certainly, were not sadistic. The men of her tribe had lost touch with their better natures, and she intended to bring them back to their senses. There was a higher standard of behavior among the Cherokee to which she intended to appeal. Nanye-hi was determined to make the men of the town see reason.

It was not a long walk from Chota to Toqua, so as soon as Nanye-hi heard the news about Sarah Bean, she was off. Walking rapidly, she reached Toqua at sunset.

On the outskirts of the town, on a high mound, a stout pole had been set in the ground. From a distance Nanye-hi could see a thin column of smoke beginning to lift into the sky, so she began to run. Little flames were already flickering around the edges of the pile of branches heaped around the pole to which Sarah Bean was tied. Nanye-hi charged through the assembled townspeople, bellowing at the top of her voice. There were, and are, no curse words in the Cherokee language, but Nanye-hi knew how to express herself quite strongly without profanity. She kicked the burning pieces of wood away from the pole, scattered the rest of the fuel, drew her knife, and cut Sarah Bean free.

> Scientists are not sure they have identified all forms of life in the park, as new species are found frequently.

Then Nanye-hi turned to the assembly: "What kind of cowards have the Cherokee men become? It revolts my being that warriors should dishonor themselves by burning a woman. Could you not fight their men so that you bring home only a woman as a prisoner? No woman captive will be harmed so long as I am Ghighau." No one dared to speak or to lift a hand as Nanye-hi led Sarah Bean back to Chota.

While she was at Chota, at Nanye-hi's request, Sarah taught the Cherokee women how to make butter and cheese. About eighteen months later, Sarah Bean was sent back to Watauga.

Several years later Nanye-hi married a trader named Bryant Ward, and her name was anglicized to Nancy Ward. In her last message as Beloved Woman, in May 1817, Nanye-hi was still urging peace and pleading that the Cherokee would develop dairy herds to supplement their food. She died in the spring of 1824 at her home near Benton, Tennessee, on the banks of the Ocoee River.

Author's note: Toqua and Chota were situated near Vonore, Tennessee, the site of the birthplace of Sequoyah. From Vonore it is only a few minutes' drive along US Highway 411 to Benton, where, on the southwest side of the little town, a parking area is located on the banks of the Ocoee River. A paved walkway leads a few yards to Nanye-hi's grave, which is marked by a small stone pyramid. Visitors often leave feathers, strips of rawhide, or arrowheads on her grave. For many people Nanye-hi is still a Beloved Woman.

1790

Stuart Bradley Finds a FRIEND and a Wife

Stuart Bradley was quite pleased with himself. His family was doing well in their home on the banks of the Watauga River, and he felt quite comfortable in leaving his siblings and parents behind so that he could go hunting. With his brothers running the farm, he could be gone for weeks at a time. People like him were called "long hunters," because of their extended jaunts into the woods. Someday he intended to settle down and get married, but for now he had a new place to hunt: the lands occupied by the Cherokee in the Smoky Mountains. Of course, this hunting place was dangerous because he had no right to be there, but the hunting was so good and the scenery so spectacular that Stuart returned time after time.

A permanent camp added to Stuart's pleasure and comfort on these trips, and he had built a good one. In what is now called the Greenbrier Section of the Great Smoky Mountains National Park, Stuart had found an overhanging shelf of rock where the bluff overhead formed a roof and one side of a shelter. He stacked stones to build the other walls needed to make a crude structure. On the front end of the structure, he constructed a small fireplace and chimney and fashioned a door made of small trees split in half and pegged together. He was able to stay dry and warm here. Stuart left his horse, which he used to pack in supplies and to pack out his meat and furs, in a thicket of cane, or canebrake, a couple of miles from his camp. With plenty of food and water, the animal never wandered far.

There were two things to keep in mind about his camp: First, a clear path would bring unwelcome visitors to his door, so Stuart always waded along a small stream to approach his camp and then stepped only on large stones to enter his shelter; second, fires were built only when fog, rain, or snow kept the smoke close to the ground (otherwise the sight and smell of the smoke would give away the location of his camping place).

One October Stuart was having a successful hunt. His comfortable shelter was becoming crowded with animal hides he was curing and meat he was preserving to keep his family warm and fed during winter. Despite his pleasure in hunting, Stuart's outdoor experience kept him alert to the skies, as he knew major weather changes could occur suddenly in the mountains.

By daybreak the rain was lashing the trees, and there were occasional bursts of sleet. By night the rain was slacking off but was still steady, and the temperature was falling. Anyone out in such weather would be in trouble, because wet clothes would lead to hypothermia, which could be deadly.

Shortly after dark, Stuart was lying propped up on his cot, listening to the storm outside and the crackling of the fire on his hearth, when the door shook. Stuart caught up his rifle and thumbed back the hammer just as the door swung back. Standing there in the ruddy glow of the fire was a Cherokee man. Water dripped from his hair and ran in streams from the sodden blanket wrapped around his body. With his rifle held steady, Stuart said, "Begone, you Indian dog, begone!" Without a word, the Cherokee closed the door and Stuart heard him walking away from the shelter. A few days later Stuart retrieved his horse from the canebrake, loaded up his meat and hides, and went home.

More than two years passed since that suspenseful night, and during that time Stuart made several more trips to his secret stone shelter in the Smoky Mountains. One March he went back, not to hunt, but to explore. Stuart was looking for a home; he was getting ready to marry and to settle down.

Stuart crossed the big mountain, presently called LeConte, and began to work his way down the hollows toward the Oconaluftee River, always alert for Cherokee and for good land. On the third day of his quest, Stuart became concerned about the weather. March had given him several days of pleasant temperatures, but that day the air felt different, and the sky was a strange pewter color. The light wind was from the southwest, but the temperature was falling. If that were not bad enough, he had been wheezing and cough-ing for the last few days, and breathing was becoming increas-ingly difficult. By mid-afternoon the first heavy, wet flakes of snow began to fall, and soon the air was so full of the swirling flakes that the trees could hardly be seen at any distance.

As a "long hunter," Stuart knew he needed protection in a dry place or else his wet clothes would suck all the heat from his body and he would die. But no shelter was to be found. Night came and visibility was reduced to nothing. The wind was colder, and Stuart, in his wet linen shirt and cotton blanket, was shivering uncontrollably. Then, ahead of him, he saw a spark, like a lightning bug in the sky. It disap-peared, then reappeared; below it, he saw a little gleam, as if firelight were shining through a crack in a door. By now Stuart was developing hypothermia and the fuzzy thinking that goes with that condition, but he still had enough grasp on reality to move toward the light. Suddenly a cabin loomed in front of him. Light was shining through a tiny crack in the wood of the door.

Stuart knocked and the door opened almost instantly. Stuart found himself looking at a face he had not seen in more than two years, the face of the Cherokee he had turned away from his hunting camp the night of the storm. The cabin seemed to whirl around him, and Stuart fell to the floor, unconscious.

For an unknown time he lapsed into and out of con-sciousness. Sometimes he knew someone was near him, but he did not know who it was. He later recalled a time when he opened his eyes and all he could see were hot coals and little leaping flames. "I reckoned my Ma had been right. She always said if I didn't change my ways, I'd end up in a fiery place. Then I realized my feet were cold, and I knowed if I had gone to Hell my feet wouldn't be cold." A hand stroked his forehead and a cup of water was held to his lips. After a long drink Stuart fell into a peaceful sleep.

Over the next several days, Stuart improved steadily. As he did, he began to take an interest in his nurse, a daughter of the household, and she took an interest in him. That summer Stuart Bradley married the young woman whose name, in English, was Yellow Flower. "Thank God," Stuart said years later, "her father was a better man than I was. I turned him away into a storm; he took me in and gave me his daughter as my wife."

Stuart had discovered one of the outstanding positive characteristics of the Cherokee. They were an open, accepting, forgiving people who were quite willing to accept into their homes and families people from other races and backgrounds. This openhearted nature would be both the strength of the Cherokee character and a typical part of their history.

The Bradley family returned to Cherokee lands to settle on a tributary of the Oconaluftee River, which bears their name. Neither Stuart nor his descendants ever forgot the kindness shown by the Cherokee.

WILMA DYKEMAN

[1920–2006]

A native of Asheville, North Carolina, Wilma Dykeman spent much of her life in Newport, Tennessee, only a few minutes' drive from the Cosby entrance to the Great Smoky Mountains National Park. Her family home was something of a small-scale nature sanctuary, surrounded by native trees and flowers. This early association with nature was an important influence on her work for the rest of her life.

Graduating from Biltmore Junior College in Asheville, Wilma attended Northwestern University, graduating as a member of Phi Beta Kappa. The year after her graduation she married James R. Stokely, a writer whose family were partners in the Stokely-Van Camp Corporation. During their courtship they had attended the dedication of the Great Smoky Mountains National Park, and Wilma soon began to write articles about the flora, fauna, and people of the mountains. These writings were published in *Harper's*, *New York Times Magazine*, and *Reader's Digest*.

In 1955 her best-known book, *The French Broad*, was published as part of the "Rivers of America" series. This was one of the first popular books to deal with the problem of pollution and the destructive effects it had on the ecology of an area. In 1966 an enduring novel about the people of the mountains, *The Tall Woman*, was released and is still in print. These books, fiction and nonfiction, drew favorable attention to the Smoky Mountains and to the unique Appalachian culture of the people who live there.

Wilma's interests as a writer were not limited to the Smoky Mountains, and her nonfiction works include two books on race relations: *Neither Black nor White*, and *Seeds of Southern Change*. For many years Wilma Dykeman (Stokely) taught a course in Appalachian history and culture at the University of Tennessee, traveled the nation as a popular lecturer, and served as State Historian for Tennessee.

1818

An Unexpected Gift

If there was one thing Lucretia Oliver had plenty of, it was solitude. Miles and miles of mountain wilderness surrounded her and there were no neighbors to talk to. Her only companions were her infant daughter, Polly, just seventeen months old, and her husband, John. Now, John was a good man, and she loved him, but he left the crude cabin early every morning and didn't return until dark. He was so tired when he returned that he could barely eat his supper before falling asleep. Polly was a treasure, but like any toddler she was always into something, so Lucretia could scarcely get her housework and cooking done.

Cooking, however, was becoming less and less a chore. Lucretia wished the family had as much food as she had solitude, because the truth was they were running out of supplies.

Back in the fall, when they had moved to their new home in the valley—the Cherokee called it Tsiyahi, or "Otter Place"—they had brought all the food they could gather, but that had not been a lot. John was not a landowner back in Carter County, Tennessee, where they had come from. He was a collier, who made charcoal to sell to blacksmiths. He had always wanted to own land, though, and when a neighbor, Joshua Jobe, offered to help the Olivers move to the valley to claim lands for both families, John had agreed.

Joshua Jobe had helped them move but then returned to Carter County soon after, leaving John, Lucretia, and Polly all alone in the wilderness. He said he would bring Lucretia a cow and a calf the next spring, but now she wondered if her family would still be alive by then.

John Oliver was not afraid of the wilderness or of much else. Under the command of Andrew Jackson, he had fought in the War of 1812 in the battle at Horseshoe Bend in Alabama, crushing the Creek Indians. Now John was fighting for land, as he had to clear it for spring planting. Every day he took his ax and went out to girdle trees, chopping the bark off in a circle around the trunk so that when spring came, the sap could not rise to the limbs, thus causing the tree to die. Because of the great number of trees, their first crop could not be planted in long, straight rows in cleared fields; rather, hills of corn and beans would be scattered among the dead trees. It was absolutely necessary that John girdle several acres of trees so that they could grow food the next spring.

Consequently, building a house became a secondary priority. The family hurriedly constructed a small cabin of logs that they left round, as they had no time to square the timbers. Building with round logs meant that large cracks were left between the logs, and chinking these cracks with mud was an unceasing chore. On one side of the little room was a fireplace built of stone, but the chimney was made of sticks daubed with mud. The floor was made of puncheons, the split trunks of small trees. The best feature of the homestead was a bold stream of water that surged up from a spring only a few feet from the door of the cabin.

When he was not girdling trees, John hunted. This was not a recreational activity but a quest to put meat on the table. Although small game was plentiful, gunpowder and shot were not, so John did not shoot rabbits or squirrels. He saved his ammunition for deer and elk. So far, he had not brought home any large animals, so Lucretia watched with a sinking heart the diminishing level of cornmeal, beans, and flour in the small barrels in which their food was stored.

Lucretia was worried about the Indians, too. There was a Cherokee village of considerable size less than 5 miles away at the other end of the valley, and John assured her, over and over, that the Cherokee were friendly. Many times he told her the story of the battle of Horseshoe Bend, where the Cherokee had fought alongside Jackson's white troops to defeat the Creeks, but these stories did not completely satisfy Lucretia, for she knew they were on Cherokee land illegally. If an Indian tried to settle illegally in Carter County, Lucretia knew that settlers would likely kill the intruder, so she worried about the Indians' reaction to their intrusion in Tsiyahi.

To make their troubles seem worse, Christmas was coming. Like the usual run of frontier folk, John and Lucretia had a great respect for religion even though their isolation meant they had no church and no minister. In the tradition of the Scots-Irish Christmas, the celebration was more than a religious celebration; it was a time of relaxation and good cheer, so far as the frontier provided those commodities. But this

Christmas of 1818 looked bleak. The Oliver family might truly starve to death.

Lucretia looked out the doorway of their little cabin and watched the snow swirl through the trees. The mountains across the valley were only indistinct shadows in the falling flakes. She worried that John might stay in the woods hunting too long and get lost in the storm. Perhaps that was him coming now, she thought, as a form loomed through the white veil of snow. Then Lucretia recoiled in horror. It was not John. More figures were emerging from the gloom—two, three, four in all. Now that she could see them more clearly, she could tell they were Cherokee.

In a sudden panic, Lucretia dashed into the cabin, slamming the door behind her. She cradled Polly in the crook of her left arm and snatched up the ax with her right hand. The little bare room held no hint of a hiding place. Her breath caught in her throat as she heard steps approach. Then feet thudded softly on the puncheon boards of the porch. No knock came at the door, no sudden thrusting against its crude panels. She heard only the gentle sounds of softly spoken words she did not understand. Then Lucretia heard the footsteps recede.

She dared not open the door for a long time, but when she did, Lucretia gasped in surprise. Under the shelter of the porch roof were four large deerskin bags. Dragging them inside, she eagerly untied the mouth of each sack and thrust a hand inside. One bag contained shelled corn. Another bag contained hickory nuts—these tough, hard-to-crack nuts were a delicacy on the frontier. The last two bags were packed with strips

of dried pumpkins. Soaked in water and then simmered over the fire, these made a dish that was both good-tasting and nutritious.

It felt as though a block of ice around her heart was melting. Lucretia had no idea why her Cherokee neighbors had walked so far through a storm to bring her and her family food. But she knew Christmas would be merrier and the New Year would hold some hope of happiness.

Author's note: More settlers began to arrive in 1819, and they soon put pressure on the Cherokee to sign a treaty giving up their lands in Tsiyahi. It is ironic that the good nature and neighborliness of the Cherokee in saving the lives of the Olivers led to a wave of settlement that eventually cost the Cherokee their homes. The Cherokees' willingness to help their white neighbors was met with rejection and even countered with attempts to take advantage of their good nature.

With the help of their new neighbors, John and Lucretia were able to build a new, sturdy cabin of squared logs. This house, which still stands, is one of the most popular stops on the Cades Cove driving tour in the Great Smoky Mountains National Park. The Tsiyahi valley became known as Cades Cove and proved to be a garden spot, indeed. The descendants of John and Lucretia were still living there when the government took their land for inclusion in the Great Smoky Mountains National Park.

1823

Sequoyah and the
TALKING LEAVES

H e knew he could do it. For all of the centuries that his people had been in contact with white settlers, the foreigners had an advantage. They could put marks on paper, send the leaves of paper across many miles, and the person who received the "talking leaves" would get the sender's message. It was time his people, the Tsalagi, or Cherokee, had this same advantage. Sequoyah thought he could give it to them.

The need for a written language had been on his mind for a long time, and he had begun working on it before he came to have such a personal desire for it. The need for writing became personal in 1813, when he and many other Cherokee men joined the army of the United States to go fight the Creek Red Sticks, the group the French called the "Baton Rouge." The Creek territory joined the Cherokee lands on the west and south, so there were long-standing disagreements over boundary lines, trade routes, and hunting grounds. At the battle of Horseshoe Bend in Alabama, under the command of Andrew Jackson, the Cherokee had made an important contribution to the destruction of the power of the Creeks.

But during the weeks and months that he and the others were away from their homes in the Smoky Mountains, Sequoyah could only watch in envy as the white soldiers received letters from their families and swapped news of their homes. Sequoyah was already at work making Cherokee a written language; now he would work harder.

Sequoyah might have seemed an unlikely figure to put the Cherokee language into writing. He was not a prominent member of the tribe, nor was he from any of the largest towns. He was born in the 1770s in the village of Tuskegee on the Little Tennessee River. His mother, Wurerth, was a member of the Paint clan, one of the seven clans into which the Cherokee tribe was divided. The father of Sequoyah was not known. Some said he was a fur trader from Virginia named George Gist; others said he was a Cherokee from a distant village. At any rate, Cherokee society was matriarchal, and his mother had important relatives, so people would listen if he could get them to support his "talking leaves" idea.

Sequoyah had taken on an enormous task. At first he tried to create a different symbol for each word in the Cherokee language. Some of the symbols he used came from the petroglyphs that prehistoric inhabitants had carved on rocks and cliffs in what were now Cherokee lands. Other symbols were copied from European languages, and still others he simply made up. Symbols accumulated on pieces of paper, on slabs of bark, even on short planks of wood. For twelve years, from 1809 to 1821, he worked away, but the project never seemed to reach a conclusion.

Sequoyah's wife was not enthusiastic about this project. Her husband had been a farmer and a silversmith, but now he spent more and more of his time in the shed he used as a study. Increasingly, the work of supporting the family fell on her. Arguing with her husband did no good, so, in desperation, one day she set fire to the shed and burned up all twelve years of work.

Sequoyah, however, refused to become discouraged. He stirred the ashes, sighed, and said he had a better idea. He then began to listen quite carefully when any Cherokee spoke in an effort to isolate the sounds that made up the spoken words. Within a few months Sequoyah had identified eighty-five vowel and consonant sounds used in forming Cherokee words. He then devised a symbol for each sound. Some of these symbols resembled letters of the English, Greek, and Hebrew alphabets, whereas others were of Sequoyah's own invention, but all of them were assigned a distinctive sound in Cherokee. This was not an alphabet but a syllabary. Now it was time to teach the people.

Sequoyah asked that a council be called. All inhabitants of the village filed into the seven-sided council house, each clan occupying a separate side. When the house was full, Sequoyah rose to speak.

> For years the white people have spoken to one another across long distances using talking leaves. Now I have learned to make leaves talk in Tsalagi. It is so easy to learn that I have taught my little daughter, only twelve years old, to listen to the talking leaves. I will show you that this is no trick.

Some of you women take my daughter, Ahyokeh, and go with her to the far side of the village. Watch her so that you can see no one speaks to her except the talking leaves.

When she has gone, one of you who doubt what I say will give me a message for her, and I will send it by the talking leaves.

There was commotion and confusion in the council house as Ahyokeh rose to her feet and left the gathering, accompanied by some women from each clan. When all was still Sequoyah asked, "Who has a message for my talking leaves?"

One man, who had been loud in his accusations that Sequoyah was practicing sorcery, spoke up. "Tell her to come here, that you are thirsty and want a drink." Sequoyah quickly wrote on a piece of paper and handed it to the man. "Take this to her yourself so that you will know there is no sorcery."

Silence fell over the council house as the messenger left to find Ahyokeh and her female escorts. Only a few minutes passed when the girl entered the room with a cup full of water. "Here, father, you said you were thirsty, so I brought you water as I came."

The skeptic was first in line to ask for lessons about how to listen to the talking leaves.

The Great Smoky Mountains receive more rain than any other location east of the Mississippi River.

Literacy spread among the Cherokee swiftly. By 1827 a newspaper, the *Cherokee Phoenix*, was in publication in Sequoyah's syllabary. Soon the Bible and hymnbooks appeared. The Cherokee never developed a literary tradition using the syllabary, but having their language in writing allowed communication between the Western Band of the Cherokee in Oklahoma and the Eastern Band in Tennessee, North Carolina, and Georgia. Such communication helped the Cherokee maintain their tribal identity in the hard years to come.

Sequoyah voluntarily migrated to Oklahoma in 1822, before the Trail of Tears. He died there in 1842 or 1843, under circumstances not completely clear while searching for a supposedly "lost" clan of Cherokee who were said to have settled in Mexico.

The syllabary developed by Sequoyah is a very efficient means of teaching reading. A Cherokee speaker can learn to read after only a few days of studying the syllabary, as compared with the several years it takes to learn to read English.

Author's note: The Sequoyah Birthplace Museum is located in Vonore, Tennessee, the site of the Cherokee Tuskegee town. The museum is open every day. Only a half-mile away is Fort Loudoun State Park, a reconstruction of the first trading post built west of the Great Smoky Mountains. A visit to these two locations makes an easy day trip from the Great Smoky Mountains National Park.

1833

A Bad Woman or
A BAD MISTAKE

rankie Silver heard the steps coming down the passage-
way, and she knew what they meant. She had long since
come to know the sound of Sheriff John Boone's footfalls.
She knew why the sheriff was coming to her cell. In just a few
minutes, he would lead her outside, where the hangman's
noose waited. Frankie Silver was to be hanged for the crime
of murder.

A year and a half earlier, on Christmas of 1831, Frankie
had gone to the home of her in-laws, Jacob and Eleanor Silver. She asked them if they had any idea where her husband,
Charlie, had gone. Her man, she told them, had gone off on
one of his extended hunting trips a few days earlier, and he
had not come back as promised. She was afraid to stay any
longer in their cabin alone, with their infant daughter, Nancy.

With Christmas fast approaching, Frankie's in-laws asked her and the baby to stay with them for a few days, but when Charlie still did not come home, his parents also became worried. A party of men went to the cabin and found no immediate trace of the missing husband, but as their search intensified, troubling items began to be found.

The fireplace in the cabin was choked with ashes, which appeared to be unusually greasy. In sifting through these ashes, a large number of bone fragments were found. The ax had numerous chips and nicks in the blade, which indicated that it had struck something harder than wood. One searcher suggested lifting the wide, thick puncheon boards that formed the floor of the cabin. Although the tops of the puncheons were scrubbed white, the sides and bottoms of the boards were stained with blood.

Suspicion began to focus on Frankie, and when, a few days later, the severed head of her husband was found in a hollow tree, she was arrested and taken to the county jail at Morganton, North Carolina. More remains were found and the Silver family held a funeral and burial for Charlie. Adding to the horror and shock felt by the community was the discovery of still more remains, so additional graves were dug until Charlie Silver lay in three separate burial sites.

Frankie's mother, Barbara Stewart, and her brother, Blackstone Stewart, also were arrested because it was believed that Frankie could not have committed the crime unaided. When Frankie's father, Isaiah, returned from a hunting trip in Kentucky, he immediately secured the release of his wife and son, because evidence against them was lacking, but Frankie was brought to trial for her life and was accused of murder.

Francis (Frankie) Stewart had met Charles (Charlie) Silver when she was about sixteen, and he was not much older.

They were married about a year after they first met and moved to an isolated area on the Toe River, just over a mountain ridge from Charlie's parents' home, an area just vacated by the Cherokee as they left their Smoky Mountain lands.

Life was hard on the frontier, but Charlie was a hard worker. Soon the materials for a cabin were collected, and neighbors came to help raise the house. It was in this cabin that Frankie and Charlie conceived their child.

Once their daughter, Nancy, arrived, Charlie seemed to lose interest in his wife. Perhaps the demands of taking care of a child, coupled with all the heavy labor of being a frontier housewife, left Frankie little time to shower attention on her husband. At any rate, the gossip along the Toe River and in the hollows was that Charlie Silver played as hard as he worked and that he played in a lot of places outside the home. Some people even said that he beat Frankie when a bad mood, or bad whiskey, was on him.

> The Great Smoky Mountains National Park was created by the people of Tennessee and North Carolina and was presented to the government of the United States as a gift.

With rumors circulating about being mistreated and abandoned by her husband, Frankie had gone to the home of the Silvers and told them their son was missing. Then blood and bones were discovered in her cabin, and Frankie was arrested.

The trial in Morganton, North Carolina, was a sensation. Only a few times before had a woman been brought to trial for murder in North Carolina, and never had there been a murder trial of a woman in Morganton. The evidence against

Frankie was strong, but questions remained: Would she have been strong enough to do the deed unaided? If she had help, who was it? Was she merely angry at Charlie for being unfaithful, or was she defending herself against an abusive husband? Under the law of the time, and according to social custom, women had few legal rights, and it was considered appropriate that their husbands dominate them.

Frankie, a mother not much more than a girl herself, aroused a good deal of sympathy among women who were beginning to question the current assumptions about their role as women. The women's rights movement would not produce a formal organization until 1848, but persons who were thinking about what is now called "gender equality" took up Frankie's cause. Letters were written on Frankie's behalf, and petitions were circulated and signed, but nothing the aroused women did swayed the course of the trial. An attempt by the Stewart family to break into the Morganton jail and rescue their daughter only made her situation worse.

The trial dragged on throughout 1832, but the probable outcome became clearer and clearer. The sentence of death was no surprise to anyone when the jury handed it down. The day of execution was to be July 12, 1833.

Now the day had come. Sheriff John Boone entered the cell with two deputies and quickly tied Frankie's hands behind her. She was led outside and was helped to climb in a cart. A patient old horse pulled the conveyance to a position beneath the limb of a large oak tree. A local minister climbed into the cart and read aloud Psalm 51. Sheriff Boone placed the noose around her neck. The legal document calling for her death was read. A whip snapped against the flank of the cart horse, and Frankie Silver died.

Immediately, legends began to develop and controversy started to spread. Was Frankie Silver a jealous wife who killed in cold blood, or was she a battered wife who had only defended herself? Did she have any last words? Did she sing a ballad from her gallows? Was she protecting her lover who had actually committed the crime? The debate continues even now. Was this the case of a bad woman or the story of a bad mistake?

Author's note: A mountain ballad recounts the fate of Frankie Silver, and old-timers sometimes argue over her motives. A novel, *The Ballad of Frankie Silver*, was written about her trial in the 1990s and legends still swirl about her spirit being seen at the site of her cabin. The three graves of Charlie Silver are located at Old Kona Baptist Church in Mitchell County, North Carolina, not far from Morganton. Frankie is buried about 9 miles west of Morganton, which can be reached from the Great Smokies by driving east from the park for about an hour on Interstate 40.

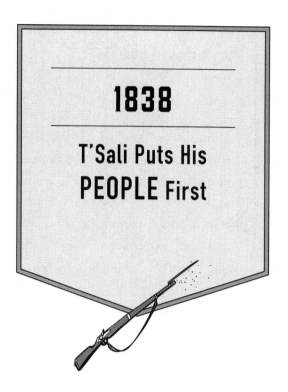

1838

T'Sali Puts His
PEOPLE First

For decades the pressure had been building: white settlers constantly closing in on the borders of the Cherokee lands, always "land hungry," always crying out for more. The settlers thought the land was wasted unless it was cleared of trees and brought under the plow. They did not understand how to live off the produce of the forest, supplemented by a few small fields of corn, beans, pumpkins, and squash. They did not farm in order to eat; they wanted to grow a surplus to sell.

Even when Thomas Jefferson was president (1801–1809), the Cherokee had been urged to go west across the "Father of Waters." Some had agreed and had voluntarily settled in the land called Oklahoma, but they had hardly arrived when the United States government told the Cherokee that they had to give up more of their eastern lands to pay for those they had been given in the West.

Now, in 1838, the end had come for the Cherokee. Their lands in Georgia had become valuable to the white man because technology had made it possible to weave cloth from cotton. The mill owners in New England and Great Britain wanted farmers to plant cotton on every acre that could be cultivated. Even the mountain lands of the Cherokee were wanted by the white settlers, because gold had been discovered at Dahlonega ("place of yellow metal" in Cherokee), and men seemed to go mad when gold was known to be present.

Soldiers of the United States Army commanded by General Winfield Scott had come into the Cherokee homeland. The task of these soldiers was to force the Cherokee to go to temporary forts until groups of about 1,000 Indians had been collected. Then each group would be sent west to Oklahoma, an event that today is known as the Trail of Tears.

T'Sali's family was among the last Cherokee families to be forced to move. Like all the Cherokee, T'Sali had a strong attachment to the land, because he believed it contained the spirits of his forebears who were buried there. T'Sali, like many of the Cherokee at this time, was a Christian, having been converted by missionaries who had distributed among the Cherokee the Bible in the syllabary developed by Sequoyah. In T'Sali's mind, being a Christian did not conflict with holding onto many traditional Cherokee beliefs. T'Sali and his family saw agreement between the teachings

of Christianity concerning self-giving and the Cherokee traditions that taught that the survival of the group was more important than the continued existence of an individual.

Because he saw no prospect of success in physical resistance, T'Sali waited quietly at home for the soldiers to come. That day came.

T'Sali, his wife, two sons, and a brother had been told in advance how to prepare for leaving, so they had gathered a few clothes and some treasured items. One pack each, plus a bedroll, was all they were allowed to take. As they left the clearing around their home, smoke began to rise from the cabin where the soldiers had set fire to it. As the sad party tramped along a trail toward a stockade, one of the soldiers became impatient with the speed at which T'Sali's wife was walking. Raising his rifle, the soldier pricked her with his bayonet.

T'Sali and the other Indian males exploded in anger. Grabbing whatever weapons they could find, including an ax, they swarmed over the soldiers. In a few seconds one soldier lay dead; the rest had fled. T'Sali and his people then headed for the mountains, where they joined a band of fugitives under U'Tsala. This group had lots of places to hide in the mountain terrain but little to eat, as the rugged mountains produced little food or game. What food they did gather they had to cook surreptitiously, lest smoke from their fires would give them away. This was a precarious existence, and its difficulties placed serious strains on the bonds that held the group together.

General Scott decided to use the stress caused the Cherokee to his advantage. In his reports to Washington, the general depicted T'Sali and his family as a very immoral group, looked down upon by the other Cherokee as outcasts. This type of propaganda would present T'Sali to the public as a common criminal rather than as a man defending his wife and home. Scott then sent a message to U'Tsala saying that if T'Sali and his sons were turned over to the US authorities to be killed, the rest of the band would be allowed to stay in the mountains.

Will Thomas, a man with a long record of befriending the Cherokee, was sent to find U'Tsala and T'Sali and to offer them Scott's bargain. A discussion broke out among the holdouts about what to do. Some thought it would be all right for T'Sali to go to the soldiers, because they thought that the good-hearted people among them would protect him. Others felt that there should be no response to Scott's offer, because they could continue to hide among the peaks of the Smoky Mountains for a long time. A few argued that T'Sali should die because his death would guarantee their safety. When it was T'Sali's turn to speak, he said simply, "We will go." He and his sons would give their lives so that a few of the Cherokee could stay in their traditional homeland.

Having given their word that they would appear at the designated place on the agreed day and, at the appointed time, T'Sali and his family went into the woods to spend their last days together. There were no guards set to watch them, no spies to look for them. An article of accepted behavior among the Cherokee was that when persons gave their word, they would do as they said.

On the morning of the day they would die, T'Sali and his sons came walking out of the woods toward the appointed place. As they passed the homestead of Abraham and Margaret Wiggins, the couple asked the condemned men to come have breakfast with them, and so they did. After resting a little, they continued on their way until they reached the point of land where the Tuckasegee River joins the Little Tennessee River. There they were confronted by their freshly dug graves. U'Tsala and his people were there, along with settlers and soldiers.

There are no overnight accommodations in the park, other than campgrounds, LeConte Lodge, and Appalachian Trail shelters.

General Scott's orders for the execution were read out, and the officer in charge ordered U'Tsala to choose a firing squad from among the Cherokee to perform the deed. At the last minute T'Sali's youngest son was saved from the sentence. But then the solemn ritual proceeded. The order was given to "make ready, take aim, fire." A volley of shots rang out, and T'Sali and his other son collapsed into their graves.

T'Sali's sacrifice was not in vain. The Eastern Band of the Cherokee on the Qualla Reservation at the border of the Great Smoky Mountains National Park owe their presence there today partly to T'Sali's unselfish deed.

LAURA THORNBURGH

[1885–1973]

Laura Thornburgh was born in Knoxville, Tennessee, only 40 miles north of the Great Smoky Mountains. A lifelong lover of books, she became a journalist even before she had completed her education at the University of Tennessee. Soon she had branched out to research and publish articles on how teachers in the local schools could be more effective. One of her innovations was producing movies with educational content; she became a nationally recognized expert on this subject. She also published books on letter writing, interior decorating, and housekeeping, but her most famous book is *The Great Smoky Mountains,* published in 1937 and still in print. Miss Thornburgh preferred to publish under the name "Thornborough," since that was the original spelling of the family name.

A cabin in Gatlinburg became Laura's summer home, and from that base she undertook frequent hikes during which she explored and photographed the mountains. When the national park began to be formed, she donated her cabin and several acres of land to the park and moved to another cabin, Burg House, outside the park boundary. She often accompanied political figures and philanthropists who were interested in the proposed park. These experiences were the research she used to write her Smoky Mountain book, illustrating it with her own photographs.

Two of the major themes explored in the book are the beauty of the mountains and the lives of the people who made them their home. It was the intention of the author to attract attention to the new national park and to provide a guide book for visitors. Although the park had become a reality by the time *The Great Smoky Mountains* was published, the book's popularity helped make the park a major destination. Thornburgh's book, along with Horace Kephart's *Our Southern Highlanders*, were perhaps the two most influential books on the formation and development of the Great Smoky Mountains National Park.

Laura Thornburgh never married, but spent her time away from the mountains with her brother and mother in Knoxville.

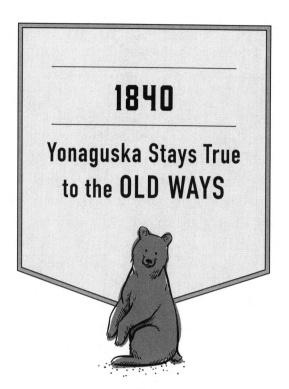

1840

Yonaguska Stays True to the OLD WAYS

Yonaguska, or Drowning Bear, as the English-speakers called him, was dedicated to the traditional ways of the Cherokee. The oral history of his people told him that for a very long time the Cherokee had lived in the mountains and valleys of the Great Smokies. Their lives were well rounded, and they did not need anything else in order to live comfortably. As far as Yonaguska could see, the Cherokee had always been a self-sufficient people.

The stories of the Cherokee also recorded how the white strangers came; Yonaguska could remember much of their coming himself. These white men brought many new things to the Cherokee lands: They brought their cooking pots of iron, which soon replaced the clay pots the Cherokee made; they brought blankets and cloth, which replaced the traditional leather clothing; they brought firearms, which replaced the bows and arrows and the blowguns, with which the Cherokee hunted. The whites also urged the Cherokee to kill animals just for their hides instead of killing only for meat. As a result of the introduction of firearms, so many deer were killed that they became scarce.

None of these things pleased Yonaguska, who preferred the old ways. But one other thing the white strangers brought did please Yonaguska, and it pleased him too much for his own good. They brought liquor to the Cherokee, and Yonaguska developed quite a taste for whiskey. As a strong young man who stood 6 feet 3 inches, he could hold a lot of whiskey before he got drunk, but, unfortunately, getting drunk became common for him. As he grew older, though, Yonaguska became more conservative and finally gave up liquor because it was not of Cherokee origin.

One white man Yonaguska did like was Will Thomas, for Will was willing to adopt the ways of the Cherokee. The bond between the two became so strong that Yonaguska adopted Will and gave him the name of Will-Usdi, or Little Will. In time, that friendship would greatly benefit the Eastern Band of the Cherokee.

In 1825 Sequoyah introduced the syllabary to the Cherokee people, which enabled most of the tribe to learn to read and write. Missionaries translated the Bible into Cherokee and as a consequence, many members of the tribe became Christians, usually Methodists or Baptists. This conversion to Christianity would be the ultimate challenge for Yonaguska.

Traditional Cherokee religion was a combination of group activities and individual morality. Events, which affected the whole village group, called for a group response.

For example, when the first corn was ready to be harvested, a dance, the Green Corn Dance, was held to celebrate the maturity of the crop and to give thanks for its bounty. The entire village was expected to participate in this ceremony either by dancing or by watching the event. Also, before men went hunting for meat, a dance would be held in which hunters acted out tracking and killing an animal.

> The wildlife in the park includes black bears. Every year humans attack bears in an attempt to rescue picnic baskets or fawns. Only once has a black bear fatally attacked a human.

Much of the Cherokee religion was a matter of personal morality, which was guided by a code of conduct handed down by stories and legends. These guidelines were followed not only because they were held to be right, but also because they were expected to be done.

The missionaries, as Yonaguska understood the issue, were telling people they should behave in a particular way because the white man's Bible said they should do so. Yonaguska did not like this idea, because it challenged the traditional ways of the Cherokee. He was quite willing for other people to read the white man's book and to make up their minds about it, but Yonaguska would be guided by the old ways.

Life for Yonaguska changed greatly as he grew older. The government of the United States forced many of the Cherokee to leave their land, an event the Cherokee called the Trail of Tears. Those who were left behind were scattered, causing the structure of the tribe to weaken. But Yonaguska still kept to the old ways.

Then, one day in 1840, a group of missionaries came to visit Yonaguska. They knew that if he agreed to become a Christian, almost all the remaining Cherokees would follow suit, because Yonaguska was seen as a leader. But they also knew that it would be hard for them to convince Yonaguska; he would have to convince himself.

Taking turns, the missionaries began to present the reasons why Yonaguska should accept the ways taught in their Bible. All day the old man sat and listened, and the next day as well. When all the missionaries had spoken, Yonaguska rose to speak. "You have told me many things you say are found in your holy book. Although your book is not a part of the Cherokee traditions, it is now written in our language, thanks to Sequoyah. Therefore, I do not choose to take your word for what the book says. I want to read it for myself."

The missionaries thought the battle was nearly won. Surely they had aroused a positive interest in Christianity on the part of Yonaguska. A New Testament in the Cherokee syllabary was quickly placed in the hands of the old man, and it was agreed they would meet at his house again in one week.

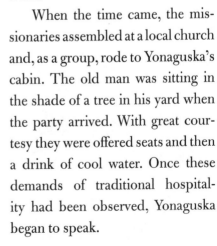

When the time came, the missionaries assembled at a local church and, as a group, rode to Yonaguska's cabin. The old man was sitting in the shade of a tree in his yard when the party arrived. With great courtesy they were offered seats and then a drink of cool water. Once these demands of traditional hospitality had been observed, Yonaguska began to speak.

"You say this is an ancient book of the white people?"

"Oh, yes," replied the senior missionary. "It was given to our ancestors many years ago, long before we came across the great ocean."

"So, then," observed Yonaguska, "for generation after generation fathers have taught their sons what is in the book and what the book wants them to do."

"That is true," replied the missionary.

"And this book tells me all I need to know and to do to be a good man?" asked Yonaguska.

"We believe that to be so."

"Well, then," said old Yonaguska, "since the white people have had this book for such a long time and since they know what they should do to be good, why is it you are not better people?"

Without another word, the missionaries left. Yonaguska continued to be true to the old ways. Thanks to him, and others like him, many of the traditional ways of the Cherokee would be preserved and continue to exist to the present day.

Author's note: The first building erected by the Methodist Church for the purpose of converting the Cherokee to Christianity was a log-cabin parsonage. The building still stands on US Route 19 East in Cherokee, North Carolina; it is currently used as a craft shop. In Campground Cemetery on US Route 441, just 2.7 miles from the road's junction with US Route 19 in Cherokee, are the graves of a half dozen of the early missionaries to the Cherokee. Yonaguska lived the last part of his life in the Oconaluftee village near the present site of the town of Cherokee.

1840

White Friend Saves the Cherokee's LAND

It was hot, sticky, and humid that July day in Washington, DC. William Holland Thomas had to concentrate on the business at hand to keep his mind from straying away to the cool heights and inviting breezes of his Smoky Mountain home. The business at hand was worth the discomfort, because Thomas was achieving a major goal in fulfilling a long-standing dream. He was about to ensure that the Cherokee remaining in North Carolina would have a permanent home.

He had left his beloved mountains and had come to Washington, at his own expense, to establish a legally binding claim to a Cherokee homeland. Now success was only the stroke of a pen away. Commissioner of Indian Affairs T. Hartley Crawford had, at long last, agreed to make Thomas an official of the Bureau of Indian Affairs. Crawford allowed him to take a census of all Cherokee remaining east of the Mississippi River and to serve as the agent to disperse almost $25,000 owed to them by the US government, a very respectable sum of money for that time.

Thomas listened as Commissioner Crawford's voice droned on, reading through the legal requirements Thomas would have to fulfill. As he listened, his mind wandered back over the years following the chain of events, which twisted like a mountain creek before bringing him to his present circumstances.

William Holland Thomas had never known his father. He was born several months after his father had drowned while crossing a flooded river on a business trip. His mother had taught him to work hard and to be honest. These qualities had earned him a job at a trading post on Soco Creek in North Carolina when he was only thirteen years old. The year was 1818. Many of the customers at the store were Cherokee, and young Will eagerly soaked up all he could about their ways and culture. His admiration of all things Cherokee was so obvious that Yonaguska, one of the most influential of all Cherokee leaders, took Will under his wing and adopted him into the Cherokee nation. There was no ceremony, just an announcement by Yonaguska. The Cherokee along Soco Creek showed by their acceptance of the young man that they approved the actions of their leader. For the adolescent Will, Yonaguska became a surrogate father. Among the Cherokee, the young man was known as Will-Usdi, or "Little Will."

Will Thomas was an ambitious young man. Like many others on the frontier, he studied law as his path to financial security and social influence. He combined the legal profession with his experience in trade to open a chain of stores throughout the Cherokee country in the Smoky Mountains. Because of his honesty, he prospered. One of the stores he opened was on the Oconaluftee River at Qualla Town, the home of Yonaguska.

Hard times were coming for the Cherokee. Gold had been discovered in the Cherokee lands of northern Georgia at a place the Indians called Dahlonega, which means "yellow metal." The first gold rush in the history of the United States was attracting hundreds of white prospectors, who saw no reason to share the bounty with the Cherokee. Outside the mountains, the Cherokee also held land well suited to growing cotton, the premier cash crop of the day. White settlers wanted that land too. Another trouble was that Andrew Jackson, president of the United States, was turning away from his old allies. He had depended on the Cherokee to help him defeat the Creeks at Horseshoe Bend in 1813, but political pressures were causing him to shun them. In anticipation of being removed from their lands, the residents of Qualla and four other neighboring towns asked Thomas to become their agent. They wanted him to help them protect their lands should the talk of a forced removal by the US government become a reality. Thomas agreed to use his legal skills on their behalf.

On December 29, 1835, a minority of Cherokee signed the Treaty of New Echota, agreeing to move west of the Mississippi River. One article of the treaty specified that any Cherokee who could be self-sufficient and who would agree to become citizens of the state where they resided could claim up to 640 aces. Will-Usdi wanted to help the Qualla

Cherokee achieve this goal, so he went to Washington to get the government to honor the relevant clause in the treaty.

In the winter of 1839, Thomas received news that both saddened and surprised him. His old friend Yonaguska had died. On his deathbed, Yonaguska asked the chiefs of the towns of which Thomas served as agent to make Will-Usdi the principal chief of the Qualla Cherokee. Agreement to this proposal was unanimous. For the first and only time in history, a man without a drop of Indian blood in his veins became chief of the Cherokee. This event was in keeping with the historical willingness of the Cherokee to accept into their midst people of other races.

All through the spring and into the summer of 1840, Will Thomas worked to convince the politicians in Washington to live up to the Treaty of New Echota. A major obstacle was that North Carolina refused to recognize the Cherokee as citizens of the state. Thomas, in his capacity as Will-Usdi, chief of the Qualla Band, saw a way around this obstacle. He was indisputably a citizen of both the United States and of North Carolina. If he became an agent to disperse funds on behalf of the Qualla Band, he could purchase lands, register the deed in his own name, and administer the lands on behalf of the Cherokee. Some men would have used such a position to become a benevolent dictator, or worse, but Will Thomas truly had the best interests of his adopted people at heart. He would try at all times to be honest to the trust he had in mind for himself.

So on a hot, sticky, humid day in July 1840, Will-Usdi carefully dipped his pen in ink and, without a quaver to betray his excitement, signed his name to the official papers. Thomas's body was in the flatlands along the Potomac River, but his heart and soul were on the banks of the Oconaluftee in the midst of the Smokies. Thanks to his work, some of the Cherokee people would be able to keep a small remnant of their lands to call their own.

Author's note: Thomas fought many more battles on behalf of the Cherokee, and during the Civil War he led several hundred of them into battle on behalf of the Confederacy. He served fourteen years in the North Carolina legislature and became an entrepreneur, promoting road and railroad construction in the Smokies. As an old man, Thomas suffered from mental illness and was a patient in the Western Hospital for the Insane in Morganton, North Carolina. He died in May 1893 at age eighty-eight and is buried in Waynesboro, North Carolina. The modern town of Cherokee, North Carolina, on the southern boundary of the Great Smokies National Park is located on the Qualla Boundary Indian Reservation and is headquarters for the Eastern Band of the Cherokee.

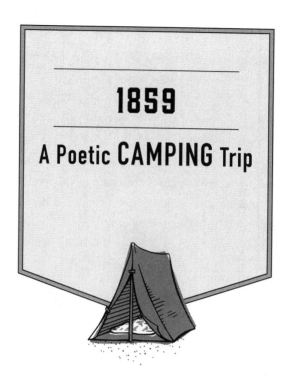

1859

A Poetic CAMPING Trip

Sterling Lanier was proud of all of his hotels, but he liked Montvale the best. A three-story frame building capped with seven gables, surrounded by sixty "cottages" for long-term guests, and set on twenty landscaped acres surrounded by 4,000 acres of virgin forest, Montvale was a magnificent property. Wealthy planters came from all over the South to spend several weeks each summer. Guests spoke of being attracted to Montvale because of the "healthful waters and salubrious air," but the presence of a French chef, a Swiss gardener, a brass band, and lots of entertainment didn't hurt at all. Free from disease-carrying mosquitoes and the worst of the summer heat, Montvale was idyllic.

Proud of his hotel, Sterling was proud of his grandson, too. Sidney Lanier was nearing graduation from Oglethorpe

College in Savannah, Georgia. He always enjoyed spending several weeks each summer at Montvale and was already showing signs of becoming the famous poet he is known as today. In the years to come, Sidney Lanier would become internationally known for his celebration of Southern landscapes in his poems "The Marshes of Glynn" and "The Song of the Chattahoochee."

In the summer of 1859, Sidney Lanier arrived at Montvale in a somewhat troubled frame of mind. The nation was feeling the stress of approaching disunion; the college debating society at Oglethorpe had already wrestled with the issue several times. Sidney arrived ready to find peace and solace from his worries about his personal future and the future of the nation.

Hunting was a favorite activity for the male guests at Montvale, and venison was frequently on the menu. (The nearby Chilhowee Mountains took their name from the Cherokee and meant "deer place.") In 1859 there were no game laws and no restricted seasons for hunting, but this year Sidney did not find hunting attractive. It was almost as if he could sense that he would soon hear enough gunshots and see enough blood to last more than a lifetime.

All summer Sidney was nervous, restlessly searching for an outlet for his feelings. The elaborate dinners at Montvale were no help, the pretty girls he met at the balls provided no distraction for him, and the walks in the woods and the fishing trips to local streams gave him no relief.

The summer season was approaching its close when one of the other young men staying at Montvale made a suggestion, which was quickly approved by Sidney and three others. Their plan was to get supplies from the kitchen, and horses from the stable, and to use pack mules to carry the equipment needed for a weeklong camping trip to one of the high peaks of the Smoky Mountains. They decided to visit Gregory Bald, and the following day they were on their way.

A "bald" in the Smoky Mountains is a high, treeless peak, something that occurs only rarely in a mountain range known for the variety and density of its vegetation. This particular bald was named for Russell Gregory, who lived in Cades Cove but drove livestock to the high-altitude pasture of the bald every summer. Before Gregory became owner of the land in 1853, the Cherokee had called the peak Tsistugi, meaning "Rabbit Place."

Gatlinburg, Tennessee, is the most frequently used "gateway" to the park; Cherokee, North Carolina, is the second most used, whereas Townsend, Tennessee, is the quiet side of the Smokies.

From Montvale, the party rode over the mountains to the valley of Abrams Creek and then followed that watercourse into Cades Cove, not far from where John Oliver had settled in 1818 (see "An Unexpected Gift"). From the floor of the cove, the heights of Gregory Bald were plainly visible. The group reached the summit by nightfall. Quickly horses were hobbled, tents were pitched, and a meal prepared.

That night after supper, the young men agreed that they would make no firm plans for their time. For the next five days, they would come and go as they pleased, wandering about the mountains in twos or threes or alone, as fancy led them. They would all return at night to eat together to prevent loneliness and to make sure everyone was all right. To Sidney, this sounded just right.

Sidney left the campsite early the next morning. He walked along the spine of the ridge, which forms the state line between North Carolina and Tennessee. The long views of wave after wave of mountain peaks helped him put the current national crisis into perspective. The cool breezes of the mile-high mountains relaxed his body, while the wildflowers, mossy stream banks, and lichen-covered rocks soothed his soul. He drank deeply at clear springs and ate the bread and cheese he had put in his pocket. That night he returned to the campsite and, after a brief explanation of his desire for solitude, moved his blankets several yards away from his friends.

Each day Sidney wandered in a different direction, and the calm of the mountains penetrated more deeply into his psyche. As the days passed, he felt more prepared for an uncertain future, and each night, by the light of his campfire, he made notes in his journals. For five days Sidney took in the healing calm of the high peaks of the Smoky Mountains. On the last night he rejoined his friends around their fire and the next day the party returned to Montvale.

The Sidney Lanier who came down the mountain was different from the young man who had gone up.

Two years later the young Sidney found himself in the midst of battle, with violent death all around. In 1864 he was in a prison camp at Point Lookout, Maryland, where men died in droves from disease. Later, Sidney would say that the memory of his days in the Smoky Mountains gave him hope and inspiration in those trying times. In 1865 he returned to a South devastated by war and with an economy in ruins. To support himself, Sidney began to write poetry, which was readily accepted by a wide audience. His famous poem

"Nirvâna" was inspired by his camping trip to Gregory Bald in 1859.

The memory of that brief, but poetic, camping trip brought peace to Sidney Lanier while he was a prisoner of war; the poem has soothed emotions and inspired imaginations for more than a century.

Author's note: Russell Gregory, a Union supporter, was shot during the Civil War by Confederate raiders from North Carolina. Sidney Lanier wrote poetry and music, played the flute with the Peabody Symphony Orchestra of Baltimore, and taught literature at Johns Hopkins University. He died of tuberculosis at age thirty-nine, having contracted the disease while a prisoner of war. Nothing remains of the Montvale Hotel except its spring and a stone walkway. These are on private property outside the Great Smoky Mountains National Park. Gregory Bald is still a popular destination for day hikes and backcountry camping. The text of "Nirvâna" is found on the Sidney Lanier website, maintained by the University of North Carolina, Chapel Hill.

JOHN HENNINGER REAGAN

[1818–1905]

John H. Reagan was born in White Oak Flats, Tennessee, today called Gatlinburg, in 1818, and lived there until he was a young man. When Texas won its independence from Mexico in 1836, Reagan moved to the new country and soon became a political leader. When Texas became a state in 1848, Reagan became a firm supporter of the Democratic Party and led their opposition to the Know-Nothing Party, an anti-immigration group. Reagan served as a judge in Palestine, Texas, from 1852 to 1857, and then was elected to the United States Congress, where he served until 1861.

When Texas left the Union at the beginning of the Civil War, Reagan was named Postmaster General for the Confederacy. He was able to convince many employees of the US Postal Service to come south and join him, as one historian put it, "effectively stealing the US Post Office." He was such an efficient administrator that the Confederate postal service actually made a profit during its time of existence.

Reagan was imprisoned for twenty-two weeks at the end of the war, but, on release, became a spokesman for reconciliation with the United States, renunciation of Secession, and granting civil rights to formerly enslaved people. His moderate approach to politics earned him the nickname "The Old Roman."

Reelected to the US Congress in 1874, Reagan served until 1887. During this time he helped create the Interstate Commerce Commission, which regulates trade and commerce that crosses state lines, and served as the first chairman of the Committee on Post Offices. He resigned from Congress to become chairman of the Texas Railroad Commission.

Reagan died at his home in Palestine, Texas, in 1905. The Reagan family name is still prominent in Gatlinburg business circles and in the surrounding area.

1860

Professor Guyot
MAKES a Map

Rain was pouring down, lightning was flashing, and the temperature was falling while the distinguished professor from Switzerland huddled under a rock ledge. Such afternoon downpours had happened frequently since he had been in the Smokies.

Accompanying the internationally known scholar was Robert Collins, a local mountain man, but the two men could barely speak to each other. Professor Arnold Henri Guyot spoke French and knew only a little English, whereas Collins spoke in the dialect of the Smoky Mountains. Although they were an unlikely pair, there existed a strange but close bond between the two men. Both men loved the out-of-doors, and both were experienced woodsmen. Guyot knew the mountains from a scientific perspective; Collins was an expert in camp lore and in local features of the hills. With only a few words spoken between them, Guyot and Collins could draw up an agenda for the day or divide the camp chores to make a temporary camp in the most efficient way. Although vastly different in background and education, they shared a passion for the mountains.

Cold, wet, muddy and hungry, the professor decided he had never been so happy in his life. He was thrilled to be surrounded by the most beautiful area of the most interesting mountains he had ever seen. His only wish was that his friend and mentor, Louis Agassiz, could have been there.

Guyot had been around mountains his entire life. Born near Neuchâtel, Switzerland, he had been attracted to the study of geology early in life and had earned a doctorate in that field at the University of Berlin, where he had become associated with Louis Agassiz in his study of glaciers. It was Agassiz who suggested that Guyot go to the United States in 1848. Guyot's fame as a geologist spread rapidly, and in 1854 he was asked to organize a department of geology at Princeton.

Now the learned professor, far away from the class-room, was doing what he loved best, tramping around the mountains. On this trip to the Smoky Mountains, Guyot was attempting to produce an accurate map of the mountains and determine the altitude of the highest peaks. Map making was no easy task in the Smoky Mountains. Although the main crest runs northeast–southwest, the lesser peaks are a jumble of heights, reaching to all points of the compass.

In drawing his map, Guyot abandoned many of the names that the Cherokee had given to various sites. He was affixing his own, because in most cases the Cherokee names had been mispronounced by the white settlers to the point that the original meaning of the place name could no longer be determined. In many instances a location had two or three names: one Cherokee, one North Carolina name based on the view from that direction, and one Tennessee name reflecting that perspective. Guyot hoped to help standardize the names.

> The song "On Top of Ole Smoky" is not about the Great Smoky Mountains National Park.

In measuring the height of the tallest peaks, Guyot was doing more than collecting facts. His measurements involved a barometer he helped design (the Smithsonian barometer), a wind vane, and a rain gauge. With measurements taken using these instruments, the height of a peak could be determined and locations chosen for the observation of weather conditions. These observation posts would become the beginning of the US Weather Bureau, the present-day Weather Service.

On this particular day Guyot and Robert Collins were working their way out to the crest where the Balsam Mountain range joins the Smoky Mountain crest. On the three-day horseback and foot trip, Guyot marveled, as he often did, at the rich soil in the hardwood coves at the foot of the mountains, where rotting leaves had accumulated for centuries. There, oaks, chestnuts, and tulip poplars reached 60 feet and more into the sky while three men would have to join hands to reach around the trunks.

As the two men climbed higher, the vegetation changed as the gain in altitude took them into a different climate and horticultural zone. At 5,000 to 6,000 feet in elevation, the hardwoods gave way to northern species such as balsam and

Fraser firs. The two men had gained enough altitude that they had made the equivalent of a trip from North Carolina to Canada, so far as the climate and vegetation were concerned.

At midday on the second day of the trek, the thickness of the bushes and the steepness of the slope forced Guyot to leave the horses behind as he and Collins continued on foot. At about the same time, Guyot observed what had become a familiar phenomenon: The morning had been clear, following a clear night. Now clouds were beginning to gather around the highest peaks.

Stopping to eat, Guyot gathered sticks for a fire to brew tea, and Collins got out bread and meat left from the night before. After a quick meal and a short rest, the men went off again under lowering skies. By half past one the rain began, and Guyot wisely sought shelter under an overhanging ledge of rock. By three o'clock the rain had stopped, the clouds were breaking up, and the sun was peeping across the mountains. Of course, water from trees and bushes soon made the explorer as wet as if the rain was still falling.

Nearing four o'clock Guyot broke out into the thinning vegetation that marked the top of the mountain. Leaving Collins to set up camp for the night, the professor set up his instruments and began to take readings. With several hours of light in hand, more light than he would have had in the valleys below, Guyot recorded most of the information he would need to determine the height of the ridge. Having done a good day's work, he was ready to go to the camp, where good smells were arising from the cooking pot and a bed of balsam boughs was ready for his repose.

The next morning the sun struck the high peak while the valleys below were still in a deep shadow. After a cup of tea and a piece of corn bread, Guyot began to explore the top of the mountain he had been climbing for the past two days. He had found no name for this location in his inquiries among the valley residents, so he hoped to find some geological feature that would suggest a name. The area atop the peak was not large, and its shape soon suggested a name. "Tricorner Knob," he wrote on his map, and so the name remains to this day. These mountains were not like the Alps, where he had grown up, thought Guyot, but he had come to love their complex beauty. He was pleased to have a role in mapping them so that more people could come to enjoy them.

Author's note: The business of mapping the Smoky Mountains would keep Professor Guyot occupied until 1881, three years before his death. During his career he founded the Department of Geology at Princeton and the Princeton Museum of Natural History, and he helped found the US Weather Service. At present, mountains bearing the names Guyot chose are found in the White Mountains of New Hampshire, the Colorado Rockies, and the Great Smoky Mountains. Appropriately, in the Smokies, a peak near Mount Guyot is called Mount Collins, named for the man who guided the professor in many of his travels in the Smoky Mountains. Tricorner Knob can be reached by following the Appalachian Trail east from Newfound Gap (US Route 441) for 15 miles. This is a two-day, round-trip hike.

1864

A Bad Day in
MADISON COUNTY

When Smoky Mountain mothers wanted to scare unruly children during the years of the Civil War, they did not call up specters of the bogeyman; they used the name of George W. Kirk. If a family was pro-Union, Kirk was merely bad news; if they were pro-Confederate, he was an ogre. Kirk, and the men he loosely commanded, represented a reign of terror in the mountains.

It appears that Kirk served for a short time in Confederate forces early in the war. Perhaps he was swept away by enthusiasm when secession occurred, or perhaps he was drafted. Certainly, Kirk was not a Confederate for long before he deserted.

In the Smoky Mountains, slavery was not a particularly divisive issue, because there were almost no slaves. Motives for choosing sides weren't as complex as in much of the nation and may have reflected nothing more than that a rival family had chosen the "other" side. The presence of old animosities meant the war in the mountains easily degenerated into a bitter, bloody affair of confrontation, ambush, robbery, and murder.

Kirk at first used his energy to guide pro-Union neighbors through the mountains to territory held by the Northern army, but he soon turned to organizing his friends to protect their neighborhoods and to take revenge on Confederate areas. Kirk found himself, more than once, battling Will Thomas and his Legion of Confederate Cherokees.

> *Elk, once found throughout the eastern parts of the United States, have recently been reintroduced into the park.*

Early in 1863 a force of Tennessee Confederates penetrated a Union stronghold in Madison County, North Carolina, and killed thirteen men and boys in the Shelton Laurel community. Later that same year, the Union army occupied Knoxville, Tennessee, and began encouraging Kirk and others to form more regularly organized military units. Soon Kirk was the leader of the Third North Carolina Mounted Infantry, a Union regiment. Even though he was only twenty-eight years of age, he was a skilled and remorseless leader of the unit. In June 1864 Kirk led his men on a raid to Morganton, North Carolina, where he demolished the train depot and broke up a Confederate training camp. Opponents swarmed around his column as he retreated. Kirk determined that his men would not be attacked successfully again. To make them an unchallenged force, he secured the best, most advanced weapons available. Within a few weeks his men all carried the .52 caliber Spencer seven-shot repeating rifle. These weapons made them more than a match for anything they met.

The small-scale, neighbor-versus-neighbor warfare led to a good deal of casual violence, and human life was held cheap. This was the background for a very bad day in Madison County.

Nancy Norton Franklin was a widow with four sons. The Confederate sympathies of the family were not strong enough to lead any of the sons into the regular Confederate armed forces, but the boys were inevitably drawn into the local aspects of the larger conflict. No doubt this included helping Confederate authorities arrest Union sympathizers and make raids on pro-Union neighbors. Bushwhacking—taking pot shots at Union units that came into the area—would also have been normal activity. As the war wore on, this activity made the boys a target for Union forces commanded by George Kirk.

In October 1864 a group of men associated with Kirk decided to "clean out" the isolated Franklin farm. They would kill the men if necessary, and they would definitely take the livestock before burning the house, barn, and other outbuildings on the place. With their Spencer rifles, Kirk's men knew that they had the firepower to do the job. Even

so, the group was quite cautious in approaching the Franklin farm; they did not want to be ambushed.

Nancy and three of her four sons—Bolus, James, and Josiah—were working at their chores when they heard horses approaching their farm. As was the case in troubled times, the males went into the house for their weapons while Nancy stood in the open yard to see who was approaching.

Bolus and James had just stepped into the yard when Kirk's men rode up. Neither side wasted any time; both immediately opened fire. The advantage was with those that fired the Spencers. Bolus and James each fired their single-shot rifles and were quickly cut down by a hail of .52 caliber slugs.

As the boys fell to the ground, with blood gushing from multiple wounds, Nancy tried to go to her sons to render any aid she could, or at least to comfort them as they died. One of Kirk's men fired at Nancy, his bullet clipping a swath through her luxuriant hair. When that failed to stop her, one of the raiders grabbed Nancy, threw her to the ground, and put his foot on her neck. Josiah, fifteen years old, had difficulty finding a weapon, but arming himself with a pistol, fired from a window, dropping a man. The Spencer rifles immediately opened fire on the house.

Had the Franklin house been built of logs, there would have been a chance for Josiah to have put up a good fight. But the house was built of boards, and the heavy lead slugs from the Spencers went right through the walls, showering splinters in all directions. Realizing that he had no chance where he was, Josiah ran out the back door and dove under the house. Hidden somewhat by the shadows and the rock pillars that supported the house, he literally made Kirk's men hop from foot to foot, plowing up the ground around their feet with pistol balls.

The pistols of that day did not use metal cartridges. Each chamber in the cylinder had to be filled with loose powder, a bullet rammed atop the powder, and a percussion cap fixed on a nipple before a shot could be fired. Josiah, however, had an extra cylinder, so after firing six shots, he quickly changed cylinders, catching some of the raiders in the open as they rushed the house. Two more of Kirk's men went down before the troop grew tired of the game of trying to spot Josiah.

While most of the group kept up a heavy barrage, one of Kirk's raiders slipped up to a window and tossed a blazing wad of hay into the house. Quickly the fire spread until the structure was engulfed. Under the house, Josiah was choking with smoke, and his clothes were beginning to scorch from the heat. No alternative was left but to die bravely, so Josiah scrambled from underneath the house, firing his last shots at his attackers. His final act was to fling his empty pistol at one of Kirk's men. Josiah fell dead with fifteen wounds, one for each year of his young life.

Such scenes were all too common in the mountains. With the loss of her house and three of her sons, this was truly a bad day in Madison County for Nancy Franklin.

Author's note: Three years after the war, one of Nancy's brothers found and killed the man who had shot at Nancy's hair. Many of the mountain feuds of later years could be traced to wartime bitterness. In 1870 Kirk was asked by North Carolina governor William Holden to lead a local militia unit to put down Ku Klux Klan violence. Kirk reverted to his lawless wartime ways and committed widespread looting and burning. Blame for Kirk's lawlessness fell on the governor, who failed to control the man he had appointed; as a result, the governor was impeached, and Kirk left the state. He died in California in 1905.

1887

Sweet Sixteen: Becky Caldwell's PLAY PARTY

Becky Caldwell was about to turn sixteen years old, and she wanted the day to be a memorable occasion. Becky lived in the Cataloochee section of the Smoky Mountains, one of the most remote areas of the entire mountain range. The name *Cataloochee* derived from a Cherokee term that means "wave after wave," an apt name, as range after range of hills and ridges roll away to the horizon. Yet in this vastness lived several families, and from among their sons, Becky would one day choose a husband.

With families living in isolation, the courting process was complicated, because there were not many social occasions at which young people could meet. But just as young girls of wealthy families in big cities had a debut, Becky Caldwell would also have a "play party." In the mountains one might have a quilting party, a pea-shelling party, a house-raising party, or such, but the focus of these types of parties was to accomplish some work. A play party was strictly for pleasure, for play. This party would give Becky the chance to invite all of the young people from a considerable distance to her home, and it would be noticed that she was ready to begin "walking out" if a young man caught her eye.

Becky and her mother, Eliza, spent several evenings discussing the guest list as they washed dishes or sat by the fire. The problem was not so much whom to invite, but how to contact them. Because there were so few young people in the Cataloochee, all of them would be invited. Not only was it important to have many guests, but also the Caldwells had no desire to hurt anyone's feelings by leaving them out of the party. The community remembered all too well the bitterness caused by divided loyalties during the Civil War, and the slightest of insults were sometimes the occasion of reopening old wounds.

> The most destructive animal in the park is the wild boar, a species that is not native to the area. Wild boar was introduced to the area in the late nineteenth century at a now-defunct hunting lodge. Some animals escaped and ever since have been causing problems by destroying native plants.

It was finally decided that Becky would invite her entire class from school, and that one of her cousins would invite all the young people from the church she attended in another valley. Eliza would let all of the mothers know that the party had her approval and that there would be enough adults to make sure none of the older boys got to "heatin' their coppers with a jug of bust-head." It was tacitly agreed that this would be a "kissing party" if a couple wanted a moment of privacy.

Now the day and time had to be set. It was decided that the guests would be asked to come about the middle of the afternoon to visit and play games. Supper would be served about sundown, and there would be games and dancing in the yard. The party would break up about midnight; the boys would go down the road to spend the night at Joe Shelton's, and the girls would sleep on pallets at the Caldwell place. Most everybody would leave early the next morning in order to be back home in time for a day's work.

Food was an important consideration. Soup and corn bread seemed the best choices. People could eat when they were hungry, and, by washing the dishes as people finished, there would be enough bowls for all. Later in the evening stack cake, with peach preserves spread between each layer of the cake would be served. Becky was promised that there would be coffee and plenty of cider.

On the big day Becky rushed through her chores so that she could get things ready. First she swept the backyard with a broom made of twigs to get rid of all the leaves and sticks, chicken feathers, and chicken droppings. Then she moved some benches out of the dining room onto the back porch and set some chairs under the chestnut tree at the side of the yard. Next she ran down to the spring branch to wash her feet and legs. For this special day she was going to wear her Sunday shoes instead of going barefoot.

But what if no one came? Becky's anxiety was relieved shortly after two o'clock when her girlfriends began arriving. Soon, nine young women were chatting and laughing when some of the boys came down the road. By half past three there were fifteen young people, more girls than boys, but some of the young men had sent word they would join the fun at dark when they finished work for the day.

The afternoon passed with the boys pitching horseshoes and the girls watching, commenting on the boys' form. As the sun went down, the soup was enjoyed, and then someone suggested a game—Snap Dragon. While chestnuts roasted in the embers of the fire, the object of the game was to see how many hot chestnuts one could snatch out of the ashes before one's fingers were burned. This game always got a lot of laughs.

The fun continued when everyone bobbed for apples. One of the boys shoved another boy's head under the water and got his whole head wet.

Then, just as the last of the boys arrived to even up the numbers, a really exciting game was suggested. Standing in a circle, alternating boy-girl-boy-girl, everyone put their hands behind them and an apple was passed around the circle by holding the fruit between one's chin and neck. This game got mouths kissably close and gave everybody a good idea about whether or not they would really like to kiss.

Next somebody suggested Spin the Bottle. Everyone got in a circle, and the person at whom the bottle was pointing when it stopped spinning had to pay a penalty. Penalties included reciting a poem, singing a song, or naming their special friend.

Becky's father had made a good-size pile of corn in the backyard, so the corn-shucking game seemed right for the next event. All the guests started to shuck corn, and when anyone found a red ear, he or she got to ask the person of their choice to walk around the house with them. Becky was thrilled when Bob Palmer found a red ear and asked her to walk with him. She and Bob were not so thrilled to find

Becky's parents sitting on the front porch, but it was rather nice when they reached the end of the house, where the chimney made a dark spot.

Now it was time to dance. Becky had two uncles who played fiddle and banjo, and her father could call sets. Soon dust was riding from all of the feet slapping on the ground, and the sounds of music and laughter rolled down the hollow. But even young people get tired when they have worked all day, and by midnight it was time for the party to end. Following the custom of the time and place, everyone solemnly shook hands before the group broke up.

Becky Caldwell had had quite a sixteenth birthday.

Author's note: The recreational and courting customs followed by Becky Caldwell and the other young people of the mountains seem quaint and innocent compared to those of today, but Becky's parents would have been considered quite liberal in providing such a party for their daughter and in allowing unsupervised "walking out" of couples into dark corners of the yard. It was through events such as the one described here that hundreds of young people over many decades found their marriage partners. The mountain people valued a good time, and their lives included as much fun as they could manage in the midst of the demanding requirements of their work.

MAYNA TREANOR AVENT

[1868–1959]

Mayna Avent is best known as an artist who painted scenes from the Great Smoky Mountains. She was named Mary by her parents but always called herself Mayna—a name which stuck for the rest of her life. Mayna grew up at Tulip Grove, an antebellum mansion in sight of Andrew Jackson's Hermitage plantation. She studied art in Cincinnati and then spent two years at the Académie Julian in Paris. In 1891 she married Frank Avent, a prominent attorney and political figure from Murfreesboro, Tennessee.

She was widely respected as both an artist and a teacher. She worked in many mediums, including oils, watercolors, pencil, and woodblock prints. Her skills were such that she was asked to restore portraits of President Andrew Jackson and other historical figures.

The Avent family spent many of their summers at Elkmont in the colony of summer residences there, but in 1918 they purchased a historic cabin originally built by the Owenby family,

one of the pioneer settlers in the area. The cabin, originally built in about 1850, became Mayna Avent's summer studio, and was modified by installing large windows to admit more light.

The pictures produced in the studio made their way into private and public collections all over the United States, including the Smithsonian and the Cheekwood Museum in Nashville, but many of them found a home with the people of the area who were their subjects, as the artist often gave the works as gifts.

Mayna was notorious for painting on any surface close to hand when the mood to paint struck her. One of her best-known paintings of Smoky Mountain wildflowers is done on a sheet of tin that happened to be lying nearby.

The Avents were strong supporters of the movement to found a national park, so it is appropriate that Mayna's studio still stands just off the Jakes Creek Trail near the Elkmont Campground.

1890

Keeping the
SCHOOLHOUSE Warm

It was dark in the woods, and cold. The morning star had not set, and the sun would not come over the ridge for a good while yet. There were strange noises in the woods as well, but nothing that frightened him; he was too much at home in the woods to be scared. He was in a hurry, and he was hungry. The sooner he reached his destination, the sooner he could build a fire, get warm, and have his breakfast.

Richard Walker was a young man with a mission. His long-range goal was to get an education. His short-term mission was to start a fire in the stove, so the one-room Little Greenbrier School would be tolerably warm when the teacher and other students arrived. One of the cruel and false stereotypes of the mountain people, then and now, is that they are ignorant and do not value education. The effort Richard

Walker was making to get an education, and the effort the community had made to provide a school, shows just how totally false that stereotype is.

It had not been easy to get a school at Little Greenbrier. Before 1882 there had been no school at all. Sevier County, Tennessee, did not think it was worthwhile to spend money to erect a building in an area where there were so few children. The parents of the Little Greenbrier area saw their children being left further and further behind the times, because there was no school. So in order to help their children, they struck a bargain. The community would put up a building and would pay a tax of $1.25 per pupil if the county would recruit a teacher. It was understood that the salary for the teacher was to be the sum total of the special tax. The more students, the larger the salary, and the longer the school year would last.

When the men of the community came to build the schoolhouse, they selected virgin tulip poplar trees whose trunks were nearly 4 feet thick and stretched 30 to 40 feet upward without forks. When these trees were felled with crosscut saws, they were trimmed of limbs, and teams of oxen dragged the logs to the chosen building site. There the logs were split lengthwise, and each half log was set on opposite sides of the building to keep the walls level in height. Due to the massive size of the trees, only six logs, split in half, were required to raise the sides of the building.

When the building was complete and furnished with backless benches and a stove, a search began for an ambitious young male student who would arrive about six o'clock every morning to start the fire, fill the wood box with firewood, and bring in a bucket of water for drinking. When he was old enough, Richard Walker asked for and got the job.

Starting the fire was a position of responsibility. School was in session only during the cold months, when the children were not needed on the farms. Cold months also meant short days, so Richard was up well before daylight.

As Richard walked toward the schoolhouse, the banks alongside the road he was walking on were covered with ice crystals, which had spewed up from the ground 3 or 4 inches high. These icy stalagmites glistened when the moonlight struck them through the tree branches. A light wind was blowing from the northwest, striking Richard directly in the face. When he came to the top of a ridge, he could see, dimly, more ridges rolling away before him. The noise of the Fighting Prong of Little River grew as he made his way west. More and more small streams made their way down each hollow to join the main body of water.

Reaching Metcalf Bottoms along Little River, Richard crossed the now large stream and started uphill away from the river. There were a couple of houses in the vicinity, and each was lit. Richard could tell that the families were just getting out of bed to begin their work for the day. He was getting close to the schoolhouse now. He had to cross the branch from the school spring several times on his final approach. This part of the trip was always in the dark, because the path led through a dense thicket of rhododendron, the footway scarcely more than a tunnel through the foliage.

There was the school, its log walls and shingle roof glinting a pale silver in the first light of dawn. Richard opened the door and walked to the stove in the center of the room. Opening a small door at the bottom of the stove, he gave a vigorous shake to the handle protruding from the grate, shaking the ashes down to the ash pan. Carefully, he lifted the pan full of ashes out onto the floor. Inside the stove a few coals

still glowed from yesterday's fire. Some shavings whittled from an old wooden shingle and a couple of pinecones were dropped on the coals, and some split pine was heaped on top of the shingles and pinecones. Before Richard had finished placing the kindling, smoke was rising, and a tiny flame flickered at the base of the fuel.

Richard took the pan of ashes in one hand and the water bucket in the other and walked outside. He flung the ashes over the bank of the little branch, which ran from the spring, and then filled the water bucket from the spring. Back inside the school, Richard set the bucket on a shelf beside the door and inserted the ash pan back in the stove. It was time to add several chunks of oak and hickory to the fledgling fire, and so he did. The room would not be warm for some time, but near the stove the chill was noticeably less. Pulling a bench close to the blaze, Richard began to eat his breakfast of biscuits and meat.

All day Richard, one of the older pupils, periodically left his seat to put more wood on the fire. The room had been as warm as its one stove ever made it, and the teacher and other pupils had been pleased with his work. At about two thirty the classes had been dismissed, and all the pupils left except Richard. While the teacher swept the floor and washed the slate board, Richard got the school ax and walked out to the woodpile behind the school. He cut and split wood and carried it inside to fill the wood box. Then he closed the draft openings in the body of the stove and dropped a large piece of oak inside so that the fire would carry through the night. Finally, with his pocketknife, he whittled shavings in case they were needed the next morning. Then, at a quarter past three, he left Little Greenbrier School for the ninety-minute walk back home. For his labor this day, Richard had earned the wage of five cents.

Author's note: The Little Greenbrier School was used as a church on Sunday, and a small cemetery was established in front of the building. At recess the children played within sight of the graves of their relatives. The building continued to be used as a public school until 1936. To reach Little Greenbrier School, drive from Sugarlands Visitor Center toward Cades Cove until you reach Metcalf Bottoms Picnic Area. Park at the picnic area and cross the river on the bridge, which carries the gravel road to Wear Cove—the only bridge, in the picnic area. At the far end of the bridge, turn right, and continue 0.6 mile to the school. From the school, the trail continues to the Walker sisters' cabin as described in the "Stubborn Old Women" chapter.

1904

Horace Kephart Arrives in the SMOKIES

The man was drunk. That was obvious to anyone who looked at him. Not only was he drunk, he showed every indication of having been drunk for a very long time. His face was not just pale; it was pasty. He shook, not just his hands, but all over like a leaf in a strong wind. His legs were beyond wobbly; they were at the point of collapse. In addition to being an obvious physical mess, the man was not as big as a minute—a thin, frail, bookish-looking fellow whose appearance seemed suited more for a library than for a tiny hamlet at the foot of the Great Smoky Mountains. His appearance did not deceive, for Horace Kephart was a librarian and a writer. He was also taking his first steps toward becoming the best-known outdoorsman in the nation. Except that just now he was too drunk to take any steps at all.

Not only was Kephart a physical wreck, he was an emotional wreck. He had left behind him in St. Louis the wreckage of his marriage and family relationships as well as the remains of an unusual career.

Horace Kephart had graduated from Boston University in 1880 and had been a librarian at Cornell for a time before going to Italy as librarian and personal assistant to Willard Fiske at the Villa Forini in Florence. After his return to the United States and his marriage to Laura Mack in 1885, he worked in the Yale library before becoming head librarian of the St. Louis Mercantile Library in 1890. While building up the holdings of that library by collecting manuscripts from early western explorers, Kephart became disappointed with the quality of writing in those accounts. Though the subject of westward expansion fascinated him, he found the accounts written by historians and explorers had no life in them. Determined not to follow in their footsteps, Kephart began writing stories about the plains, hunting and fishing, and other outdoor subjects. He also began to express disgust with materialistic urban life and to take long, solitary trips into the Ozark Mountains of Missouri and Arkansas. This was also the time when his drinking problem began.

In 1904, in an attempt to find his mental and spiritual bearings and to preserve the relationship he and his family still valued, Kephart decided to, as he said, "go to the back of beyond." Using a map, he looked for the largest blank space he could find in the eastern United States. His choice fell on the area in North Carolina and Tennessee called the Great Smoky Mountains. Packing a minimum of clothing and camping gear, he set out for his new life. Through a friend, Kephart made travel arrangements. His train was to be met at

Bushnell by Granville Calhoun, a man he did not then even know.

Calhoun recalled meeting the train that brought Kephart to the Smokies. The train discharged several people, most of whom quickly left to go about their business. When only one was left, Calhoun approached him, knowing even as he saw him that the frail-looking fellow was drunk and that it must be Kephart. The trip to Calhoun's home in Medlin had to be made on muleback, and Kephart could barely get on his mule and stay on it. He certainly could not control the animal, so the pair slowly ambled along. Calhoun did not want to be overtaken by dark on the rugged mountain path, so he kept urging Kephart to go faster. When no response was

forthcoming, Calhoun took the reins of both mules and gave Kephart's animal a swat with his hand. They then made good time covering the 16 miles from Bushnell to Medlin, but Kephart had to hang onto the saddle horn, the mule's mane, and anything else he could get a hold on. By the time the Calhoun home had been reached, Kephart was no better than a lifeless corpse; indeed, Granville Calhoun said he thought he had a dead man on his hands. He had to be carried to his room and put to bed. When asked about food, he muttered that a soda cracker and a glass of water sweetened with a little sugar were about all he could manage.

Not willing to have a guest in his house die of hunger, Calhoun went to the cellar and got a two-gallon jug of strawberry wine his wife had made and poured Kephart about half a water glass full. The smell alone revived the prostrate guest enough to drink the wine and ask for more. Calhoun knew about giving a drunken man "a hair of the dog," and he also knew about beginning another binge, so he said no to the request but promised him another drink later. Following the second drink an hour or so later, Calhoun insisted on milk. Later, Kephart would recall little of that day, but the bouquet of the strawberry wine stayed with him for many years. The milk soon gave way to milk with corn bread crumbled in it, then corn bread with butter, and, finally, vegetables. Good food and abstinence began to remove the alcohol from Kephart's system.

> Though now almost extinct, American chestnuts were once the dominant trees in the Smokies, both in number and size. A single chestnut tree could once produce more than a thousand pounds of nuts for families of the Great Smoky Mountains.

As soon as he was physically able, Kephart went into the remote reaches of the Smoky Mountains. For three years he lived alone on the North Carolina side of the mountains, sometimes in a tent, sometimes in old cabins or buildings at one of the abandoned copper mines, which dotted the mountains. Although almost every hollow had in it someone who made whiskey, by sheer willpower Kephart had overcome that temptation. In the solitude of the mountains, he recovered his grasp on life. His drunken days were behind him.

Eventually he would take lodging in Bryson City, North Carolina, but he would go into the mountains for extended periods, coming back to write of the people he met and of the scenery that surrounded him. With these writings Kephart became the first (and is still the greatest) of the tellers of tales about the mountains—their flora and fauna and their people. His hunting and fishing stories won him fans all over the United States and Canada, and he became recognized as an expert in the subject of sporting firearms.

Kephart's descriptions of the people and the mountains helped spark the drive to establish a national park. The mountains preserved Kephart; it is only appropriate that he helped preserve them.

Author's note: Bushnell no longer exists. It was one of the many tiny crossroads hamlets flooded by the construction of Fontana Dam during the days of World War II. Mount Kephart, one of the highest peaks in the Smokies, is an appropriate memorial to the outdoorsman and author. Kephart Prong Trail begins at a parking area on the Newfound Gap Road 3.7 miles from Smokemont Campground and leads to Mount Kephart Shelter. This is a 4-mile round-trip. By following the road signs from Cherokee to Fontana Village, one can reach more Kephart country. A boat from Fontana Village will deposit hikers at Hazel Creek Bay. From there hikers can follow the Hazel Creek Trail to the Sugar Fork Trail, the location of the settlement of Medlin, where Granville Calhoun took Kephart in 1904. This hike is approximately 10 miles, round-trip, not counting the boat trip across the lake.

1912

Gatlinburg Saves
Its School

A humble little log cabin stands at the busiest intersection in Gatlinburg, Tennessee, the town that has the most-used entrance to the Great Smoky Mountains National Park. This tiny building is not given a second glance by the majority of the millions who visit the park annually, but without this tiny cabin the park would be a vastly different place.

The cabin stands on the grounds of the Pi Beta Phi Crafts School, adjacent to the Arrowmont Craft Shop. The school is one of the premier institutions in the nation that teaches both traditional and innovative techniques to artists and crafts-persons. Insofar as the park emphasizes traditional mountain ways, the Pi Beta Phi School has been responsible for helping shape the park by encouraging traditional mountain crafts. But had it not been for the events that occurred one day in 1912, the school would not have existed.

In 1910 Pi Beta Phi, the nation's oldest collegiate fraternal organization for women, sent representatives to Gatlinburg to start a school. The tiny, isolated village had been chosen because it lacked educational opportunities more than any other place in the Appalachian Mountains. It was not that the mountain people did not value education; rather, opportunities for schooling were slim. Families lived far apart along tracks so crude they could hardly be called roads. This meant it was impossible to get enough children together in one place and time to conduct school lessons. Even when enough students were gathered to support a teacher's salary, bad weather, for example, might make travel to school impossible. During the spring and fall, children were needed to help with planting and harvesting crops. Although several families clustered around the village of Gatlinburg, the place itself was quite isolated. Travel west, south, and east was blocked by the Smoky Mountains. To the north, Sevierville, the county seat, was less than 20 miles away, but this was a full day's journey in dry weather; in wet weather it was not advisable even to attempt the trip.

All over the United States, the opening decades of the twentieth century saw a social movement spreading that was based on reaching out to both urban and rural poor people. But in coming to Gatlinburg, the teachers sent by Pi Beta Phi faced an unusual challenge. These women were outsiders and, as such, were under suspicion. Had they really come to help, or were these "fotched on" women coming to "ruin the chillen" by putting "fancy idees" into their heads?

An unused school building in Gatlinburg, at the point where Baskins Creek entered the Little Pigeon River, along with an adjacent "cottage" to house the teachers, became the first outpost of the "Pi Phis" in the mountains. Soon the women were teaching basic literacy to some thirty youngsters and were demonstrating hygiene, meal planning, and home-making skills all around the mountains. They also began to urge a revival of traditional crafts, especially weaving, as a way of bringing some money into the lives of the mountain people, some so poor they lived on a barter economy.

Although Gatlinburg and the Smoky Mountains were isolated, modern merchandising had penetrated the hills. Ready-to-wear work clothes and cloth for shirts and dresses were available in the three general stores in the village at affordable prices. Because so much work was involved in spinning and weaving, these traditional skills were among the first to be abandoned in favor of more modern ways. By 1910 the craft of weaving was remembered only by a dwindling handful of elderly women. Although no one wanted to go to the work and effort of weaving cloth to make clothes for their families, there was a tourist market for some traditionally made items. The intricate weaving of some patterns, coupled with the soft colors of the traditional vegetable dyes, made homespun counterpanes very attractive to tourists, if a wide enough market could be reached.

The first market for the traditional crafts would be the summer visitors. Two establishments, Andy Huff's Mountain View Hotel and Dick Whaley's Riverside Boarding House, drew tourists during the summer months, and more travelers were hoped for. But despite the school's contributions, local support for tourism was slow to develop.

After some two years Pi Beta Phi gave Gatlinburg an ultimatum: They wanted seventy acres owned by Eph Ogle on which to build a bigger and better school. The price initially asked was $1,800, which Ogle would reduce by $250 as his donation if the rest of the money could be raised. The national office of Pi Beta Phi would contribute $600, but the rest of the money would have to be pledged by the local community by a set date or else the school would close.

> Two species of poisonous snakes are found in the park, the timber rattlesnake and the copperhead; however, they are very shy and are seldom seen by visitors.

The announced day drew near, but there was little excitement or comment in the community about the school closing. On the day the decision was to be implemented, a wagon arrived from Sevierville to haul away the school equipment and the teachers. Galvanized by the imminent loss of the school, a local woman, Mrs. Andy Huff, sent word to her husband, who was cutting logs out in the woods, to get busy and save the school that their children attended. Soon Andy and one of his logging partners, Steve Whaley, came to the general store, which was the community gathering place and pledged $250 each. This was a large sum of money for that time and place, but the total was still short of the amount needed.

Because of the strong value the community placed on education, carefully hoarded cash was brought out of its places of safekeeping and counted. Shrewd estimates were made as to what could be spared. In amounts as small as 25 cents, the money trickled in. The children who attended the school were full of wonder and excitement over the fate of the school, but true to the code in which they were reared, they remained outwardly impassive. Disappointments were so common in the lives of the people that they were taught to hide their emotions and not to expect too much.

The shadows were getting long as the sun went behind the western ridges. The wagon from Sevierville was packed, and a closed sign was ready to be nailed to the school door when an excited messenger came up the hill from the store to the teachers' cottage. The message was that all the teachers were invited to come down to the store.

Although it was a weekday and the weather was suitable for outdoor work, the store was jammed with men watching and commenting on the funds being raised for the school. As person after person came into the store and quietly put his or her contribution on the table, tension mounted. At last a smile spread over the face of Eph Ogle. The needed sum of money was stacked on the table. Grinning from ear to ear, Ogle handed the school chairman, Elizabeth Helmick, the title to the land. Education had come to Gatlinburg to stay.

Author's note: Artists and craftspersons from many states and nations come to the Pi Beta Phi School. The campus in the heart of Gatlinburg includes workshops where the craftspersons can be observed at work. There is a public gallery where completed work is displayed and a craft shop with items for sale. Public schools long ago took over the educational function of Pi Beta Phi in Gatlinburg, but the endurance of the old craft tradition in the area surrounding the national park is an enduring legacy of the influence of the group. Huff, Ogle, and Whaley are still prominent names in Gatlinburg. Because of the real estate development brought about by tourism and the national park, these families are still mountain folks, but they are far from poor.

ARTHUR J. STUPKA

[1905-1999]

There are many unsung heroes who have made the Great Smoky Mountains National Park accessible to the public, and one of them is Arthur John Stupka. The world-renowned biodiversity of the park was discovered, cataloged, and made available in easy-to-understand books by Stupka, the first naturalist sent to the Smoky Mountains by the National Park Service.

Stupka was born in Cleveland, Ohio, to parents who had emigrated from what is known today as the Czech Republic. He earned BS and MS degrees from Ohio State University, and was hired by the National Park Service, working as a naturalist at Yosemite and Arcadia National Parks before being assigned to the Great Smoky Park in 1935.

Stupka's initial greeting at his new assignment was unusual. Park superintendent Ross Eakin told him, "I don't need a naturalist because I don't want more visitors until construction is finished. Go roam around the park." Stupka was thrilled; he had almost a half-million acres of mountains and woods to explore, and he got paid to do it.

From his first day in the park Stupka kept carefully written journals about what he saw and found. Soon he was cataloging a list of "firsts" found in the park, including plants and animals found nowhere else. This careful observation and cataloging brought scientists from all over the world to study the Smoky Mountains and their life forms.

Stupka did not associate only with scientists; he was also a favorite with the general public, leading nature walks, conducting evening programs at campgrounds, and writing nine books describing the flowers, shrubs, ferns, and other natural inhabitants of the park. Even after his retirement in 1964, Stupka kept up his walks in the park, recorded findings in his journals, and talked with park visitors.

Arthur Stupka died in 1999. In 2007 a research collection at the Twin Creeks Science and Education Center in the park was named in his honor.

1915

A Mountain Girl's Wedding Day

Dorie Cope was born in the Smoky Mountains, and except for one or two brief intervals, she lived among them until she was a middle-aged woman. She had many good times in the mountains, but her most memorable day was the day she got married to Fred.

Dorie Woodruff was fifteen years old when she met Fred Cope, her future husband. At first Fred, age twenty, was attracted to Dorie's best friend, and Dorie was too shy to even talk to him. Once Fred teased her about being so shy, and Dorie's response was to call him an unprintable name. Much to her surprise and chagrin, Fred came to her home a few weeks later to become a boarder.

Dorie's mother was so busy cooking, washing, and cleaning for their eight male boarders that she didn't notice that her daughter was falling in love. "Dating" in the traditional sense was not a mountain custom because there was no place to go, so young people "walked out" instead. There was no privacy at all in the Woodruff home, crowded as it was with eight boarders and three family members. Dorie and Fred "walked out" into the woods to talk or to pick bouquets of wildflowers. Fred liked to fish, but Dorie did not, though she would sit on the bank of the stream while Fred angled for trout. Secretly, Dorie and Fred made plans to spend the rest of their lives together.

One late spring day Dorie, now sixteen years old, announced her intention to marry Fred. Her announcement caused quite a scene, for Dorie's mother had not married until she was twenty-three years old. Besides, all parties concerned knew that Fred's parents would oppose the marriage, for they were "town folks" who had some education, liked music, and held white-collar jobs. But love won out despite their opposition and the wedding day was chosen.

Dorie and her family lived in the Fish Camp Creek Lumber Camp in what is now the Great Smoky Mountains National Park. In the camp there were no churches and no preachers, so in order to get married, she would have to leave home. On the Friday before the wedding day, Dorie went to Gatlinburg with a relative and then on to his farm. On Sunday Fred arrived on the relative's farm in a borrowed team and buggy. Together, they drove back into Gatlinburg to find a preacher but without knowing just where they would find one.

As their horse clopped down the single muddy street of the little village, another horse came round a bend toward them. By good fortune, Fred and Dorie discovered that the rider was a local Baptist preacher, hurrying from the church where he had just delivered a sermon to a building where another congregation awaited him. Dorie and Fred flagged down the parson, and without his dismounting or their leaving the buggy, the vows were said. In the middle of Gatlinburg's only street, Dorie was wed!

> Canadian juncos do not migrate from the Smoky Mountains to Canada for the summer; they simply fly to a higher elevation a few miles away.

What now? Fred had no money for a honeymoon, not even any money for a wedding dinner. There was only one restaurant in Gatlinburg at that time, the Mountain View Hotel, and it served only hotel guests. Even Ogle's general store was closed on Sunday, so the newlyweds could not get even cheese and crackers for their lunch. Married life is full of surprises, the couple realized. The excitement of getting married had driven all thought of what came next out of their heads. Tired, hungry, and a little let down, the couple made their way back to the boardinghouse run by Dorie's parents. Supper that evening was a quiet affair, with the usually boisterous men strangely silent. Even stranger, after supper the men all slipped away into the darkness, and Dorie's parents disappeared into the kitchen. An awkward silence ensued before Dorie excused herself and went to her bedroom to put on her nightdress. As soon as she was under the covers, Fred came in, put on his nightshirt, and only then took off his pants, before slipping into bed and blowing out the lamp.

Seconds later the door crashed open. Whooping and hollering, boarders, parents, neighbors, and friends filled the room. Cowbells rang, guitars and fiddles sang out, and tin pots were beaten with sticks—a din that announced the beginning of the old custom of shivaree, a traditional way of celebrating a wedding in the mountains.

Shivaree is a corruption of the Latin word for "headache," and there was enough noise to cause one. All the men trooped to Fred's side of the bed, snatched off the covers, and hoisted him aloft on their raised arms. All the women swooped down on Dorie. A parade formed outside, and Fred, now seated straddling a fence rail, was carried off into the night while Dorie found herself in the kitchen with food covering every level surface. The idea behind the shivaree was to separate the bride and groom at the beginning of their wedding night and to threaten to keep them apart all night.

All the neighbors brought something to eat. There were apple pies, peach pies, blueberry pies, pumpkin pies, and sweet-potato pies. There were deep-dish cobblers and bowls of fruit from those neighbors who still had a few fresh apples in their cellars. There were pots of coffee, not the weak "grain of coffee to a gallon of water" variety, but a rich, strong, black brew. Outside the house there was something else to drink, which was of the clarity of water even if its chemistry was quite different. But the centerpiece of the feast was the cake.

This was not the spun-sugar, butter-icing wedding cake

of today with a bride-and-groom figure on top; it was a stack cake. Sugar was scarce in the mountains. Butter and eggs could be sold (this is why the pies were the type that had no meringue), so the cakes were not iced. Instead, a single thin cake was baked, and then another layer placed on top,

then another, and another. Between each layer was jam or mashed fruit, and more of the same would top the last layer and run down the sides of the stack. The taller the stack, the more important the event. Dorie was quite pleased with the height of her cake.

People filled their plates, and soon jokes and banter flew all around the boardinghouse dining room. Many of the jokes were earthy, if not bawdy, because everyone present lived close to nature, and the ways of a man with a woman was no mystery to any of them. Wherever guitars and fiddles were to be found, dancing soon followed. This was not the "sinful" round dancing of the flat country where a man put his arms around a woman, but wholesome, old-fashioned square dancing. Boots slammed onto the floor, shoes patted against the boards, and the entire house rolled on its foundation, rocked to its rafters with joyful noise.

Monday, however, was a workday, and, finally, the crowd began to thin until, at last, Dorie's wedding day became her wedding night. The most memorable day of Dorie's young life came to a close.

Author's note: Fred and Dorie had ten children. In 1943 they followed the path taken by so many Appalachian families, moving to the city to work in a factory, filling one of the numerous wartime jobs. Dorie's full story is affectionately told by her daughter in *Dorie: Woman of the Mountains.* To some people, there may seem to be nothing notable about the wedding day of Dorie and her life with Fred, yet theirs is the story of untold thousands of mountain couples who grew up among the hills of the Smokies but who had to leave to make a living. Although living away from the mountains, the hearts of these people remain in their beloved hills. As Dorie and Fred show, ordinary lives are often quite remarkable.

Nothing remains of the Fish Camp Creek Lumber Camp but the stream, often called Fish Camp Prong. The stream still flows near Silers Bald, one of the high mountain peaks on the Tennessee–North Carolina state line.

1920

Decoration Day
in Cades Cove

Competition for members was intense among the various churches that dotted the Smoky Mountains. The field of possible converts was not large; most families attended the same church or, at least, a congregation of the same denomination, generation after generation. Occasionally, when a marriage took place, one of the spouses would join the other spouse's place of worship, but most people were loyal to the church they had always attended.

The doctrinal differences between the churches in the Great Smokies might seem tiny to an outsider, but to the members these differences were weighty matters indeed. Was it necessary to send missionaries to foreign lands to preach the gospel, as the Missionary Baptists claimed, or would an all-powerful God convert whomever he chose without human intervention, as the Primitive Baptists averred? Was true baptism by immersion only, as all the Baptists agreed, or were the Methodists correct in accepting sprinkling as a valid mode for administering the sacrament? Such issues sparked many a furious debate in the coves and hollows of the Smokies, with Bible verses quoted on all sides of the issues.

Nowhere was the religious rivalry more intense than in Cades Cove, where Missionary Baptists, Primitive Baptists, and Methodists lived together as neighbors and where the church buildings of each of these groups stood within sight of one another. But even in Cades Cove, the rivalry was put aside one day each year for Decoration Day, when the motto was "Let us come together as Brothers and Sisters in the Lord."

Decoration Day is a very old Southern tradition, whose origins have been lost in time. In the days before modern conveniences, such as lawn mowers and weed trimmers that make lawn work look easy, graveyards were not always neatly kept. Only in spring was the grass scythed and raked, bushes and hedgerows trimmed back, gravestones reset (if a formal stone was present on the grave at all), and flowers placed on the graves. This time-consuming work was performed on the weekend, but it was a time of celebration, during which the participants brought food to a central location. They ate together while exchanging stories and memories about the relatives and friends whose graves they were tending. Sermons and gospel singing were usually part of the event as well.

In Cades Cove three such days—one for each church— made no sense. Besides, most families had cousins and friends buried in graveyards at each of the churches. As a matter of simple pragmatism, as well as an example of community unity, all the Cades Cove churches came together for a common Decoration Day. The event of 1920 was a typical example.

As the last Sunday in May—the traditional date for Decoration Day—approached, the men got out their tools and gathered to survey what work needed to be done at each graveyard. On the Friday before the big day, family members from Maryville, Knoxville, and Asheville began to "come in home," the mountain expression for arriving. Meanwhile, the women were busy cooking and baking. Each woman's reputation, and that of her church, was based on what came out of her kitchen.

Saturday morning the work of cleaning the graves began with the men and boys working as a group, cutting brush and grass and re-mounding the graves with fresh dirt. Dead trees had to be removed. It was a matter of great pride to be chosen as the ax-man responsible for felling the tree before it could damage the gravestones in its path. At noon invitations were extended to "come home with me and eat dinner." By late afternoon all the burial grounds had a neat appearance.

The women spent Saturday finishing the cooking, getting "Sunday clothes" ready for church services, and gathering flowers from the yards and from the woods. One reason for having Decoration Day in May was to take advantage of the abundant wildflowers blooming at that time.

On Sunday morning families made their way to the Missionary Baptist Church. Trucks and cars were on the road, but many families still made their way in wagons or buggies. Once at the church, groups made their way to the graves of friends or relatives, placed flowers on the freshly tended mounds, and gossiped and reminisced about the departed. When the church bell rang, all filed inside for a program of speeches, gospel songs, and scripture readings. Laypeople led much of the Decoration Day services in each church. Although the pastor might be a beloved figure, his authority was kept carefully circumscribed during Decoration Day.

> Once almost displaced by rainbow trout, the native brook trout are now making a comeback with help from the Park Service.

To be chosen as a speaker on Decoration Day was an honor; only men with the best reputations for oratory were asked to talk. When the Missionary Baptists' best orators were finished, the crowd moved in a mass to the Primitive Baptist Church, where yet another program was offered. Although the format was much the same as the first program, the speakers all tried to relate stories and anecdotes relative to the people who had attended that church. The Primitive Baptist Church was the oldest religious institution in the Cove, tracing its roots back to 1827. Many of the earliest Cove settlers, including John and Lucretia Oliver (see "An Unexpected Gift"), were members, and the church enjoyed great esteem locally.

Because the local school was "neutral ground," the noon meal was spread there, and a spread it was, indeed. The dinner interval was two hours in length, and no one wanted to insult the cook, so most everyone tasted every dish on the tables that were out under the trees. Only after the last morsel had been eaten, and the sparse leftovers put away, did the crowd proceed to the Methodist Church.

Those Methodist men must have been mighty orators to keep the audience awake after such a meal. Lively singing by quartets, some local and some from outside the Cove, helped banish drowsiness. The program lasted until the shadows began to grow long toward the east and it was time to go home to "do up the night work" around the barn and care for the domestic animals.

At all the programs, talks and sermons dealing with disputed points of doctrine were banished on this day. The occasion was meant to be one that used the golden cords of memory to bind together all the residents of the Cove as brothers and sisters.

Author's note: Decoration Day is still commonly observed in rural churches throughout the mountains and all over the South. The Methodist and Baptist churches in Cades Cove are marked stops on the loop road through the Cove.

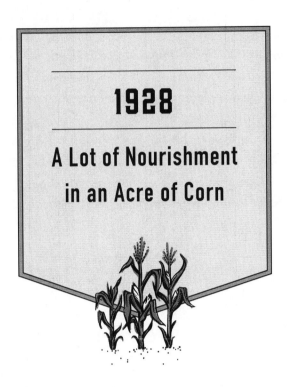

1928

A Lot of Nourishment in an Acre of Corn

Susan Vanmeter was not accustomed to thinking of herself as a "romantic" figure. Even though she had gotten involved with another man following her husband's death, it was not romance that had brought her into the relationship with John McIntyre; it was whiskey. Making whiskey was a long-standing tradition in the hills and hollows of the Smoky Mountains, but it was not respect for an old custom that had brought Susan and John together; it was simple economics.

Traditionally, whiskey had been made in the mountains to serve as one of the chief medicines the people possessed. Whiskey making later became the solution to the transportation problem that plagued the mountains because only rough roads led into and out of the heights. A bushel of shelled corn weighs fifty-five pounds; however, three bushels of shelled corn (165 pounds) produced one gallon (nine pounds) of whiskey. This reduction in weight and bulk helped solve the transportation problem.

After 1863 whiskey was made in secret because the US government placed a tax on distilled liquor and the mountain people did not feel they made enough money out of their whiskey to afford to pay the tax. In 1920 the United States adopted the Prohibition amendment to the Constitution. This created a market for mountain whiskey because it was now the only kind obtainable. The Internal Revenue agents, or revenuers, were determined to enforce the law against making and selling mountain whiskey.

When Susan's husband died, she found herself struggling to make ends meet and did not see much hope for doing any better from the ten acres to grow corn on that her deceased husband had left her as his only legacy. When John McIntyre came to her farm, she supposed he had romantic intentions and wanted to determine if she was ready to remarry. For lack of any other topic of conversation, they began to talk about her crop of corn.

John remarked that there was a lot of nourishment in an acre of corn, but Susan responded that it was true only if a person liked to eat corn bread all the time. John slyly commented that there was more than one way to cook corn. Gradually the conversation led to the revelation that John was proficient in making whiskey, having learned the skill from his father. He also owned a good still in a suitable location—on a remote spring branch in a hollow high on the side of one of the mountains. The entire operation was sheltered by a weather-tight still house.

John explained to Susan that the process began with shelling corn and placing the kernels in sacks immersed in warm water. When the kernels were thoroughly soaked, the sacks were left in a warm, moist place until the kernels began to sprout. The sprouting kernels, which contained a fairly high sugar content and natural yeast, were then cracked or coarsely ground. Mixed with more warm water in a barrel or vat, the mash was left to ferment for several days until the desired alcohol level was reached. John determined the alcohol content by the scientific method of dipping a finger into the mash and tasting the liquid.

When the mash was ready, it was poured into the pot, as the copper boiler of the still was called. The top was placed on the pot, and the closed still was set on a firebox. A spiral copper tube called the worm led from the top through another barrel, which was filled with cold water. The fire boiled the mash in the pot, producing steam. The cold water surrounding the worm condensed the steam to liquid as it ran through the thumper, as the barrel filled with water was called. When all the mash had been cooked, the resulting first run, or low wine, had to be redistilled to get rid of fusel oil and other undesirable quantities. Only after a second run through the still was the high wine ready to drink.

As John pointed out, a good deal of labor was involved in making whiskey. Once the mash began to be cooked, the process could not be stopped. The cooking had to continue night and day until finished. Then there was the difficulty and danger of getting the whiskey to market.

After listening to John describe the process, the work, and the dangers, Susan was still attracted by the profit to be earned, so she became partners with John in making whiskey. They agreed that she would provide the corn from her crop, John would provide the still and the expertise to make the whiskey, and they would divide the money earned.

John began cooking the mash when the weather turned warm and dry. The high humidity, which contributes to the smoky nature of the mountain atmosphere, gave way to bright blue skies. This change in the weather, which caused the smoke from the fire in the still house to raise high into the clear sky, brought the downfall of John and Susan.

Shortly after dinnertime, one o'clock for most mountain people, Susan heard the call of an owl from down the hollow. She knew that this was a signal from a friend that strangers were in the area, because no owl calls during daylight. A little later, from a house even closer, came the sound of a bell ringing at a time when bells never rang. Then her dog began to bark, so Susan took her rifle and silently disappeared into the woods. She was sitting on a log when she first saw the men. They were on the far side of a pasture, about a dozen in number, and they were splitting into three groups, preparing to move up the mountain in such a way as to surround the still house where John was at work.

One group of men went wide to Susan's left into the woods, another group went out of sight to her right, and the remaining group came directly toward her. When the men were 50 yards away, just at the pasture fence, Susan brought her rifle to her shoulder and fired. A sure shot, Susan expected the men to fall. Instead, the top rail of the fence exploded in splinters. She had forgotten to correct her aim for shooting downhill! Before she could aim again, the men were all under cover. While some kept her pinned down with gunfire, the others crept closer to her position. Soon the men were all around her, and she had no choice except to throw down her rifle and raise her hands in the air. When the lawmen and Susan reached the officers' car, John was there also, in handcuffs.

A few weeks later Susan stood before a judge. Much to her surprise, he expressed much the same sentiment that she and John had held. There was indeed a lot of nourishment in an acre of corn. Susan would be able to eat for the next eighteen months off her crop. Unfortunately, she would take her meals in the Women's Prison in Nashville as she served her sentence for aiding in making illegal whiskey.

Author's note: Nowadays, moonshine whiskey is the subject of jokes, tall tales, and ballads, but at the time when making whiskey was a common activity, it was no more funny or romantic than is the contemporary drug trade.

MARGARET STEVENSON

[1912–2006]

Margaret Stevenson was not born in the shadows of the Great Smoky Mountains. Her parents were Christian missionaries to China, and she was born in the city of Kuling. The family returned to the United States when Margaret was a child, in part due to her poor health. In 1930 she enrolled in Oklahoma State University, graduating Phi Beta Kappa in 1934, and then did graduate work at the University of Pittsburgh. In 1936 she married Reverend William R. Stevenson, a Presbyterian minister, and they served churches in the Maryville, Tennessee, area.

Still plagued by ill health, Margaret decided to transform her life by becoming physically active. At age forty-five she began hiking regularly in the Great Smoky Mountains National Park. At age forty-eight she made her first hike up Mount LeConte, a trip she would repeat 718 times until her final trip in 1997, when she was almost eighty-five years old. When Margaret was in her mid-fifties she was truly hitting her stride, so to speak. Her hiking diary for one October hike records:

Elgin and I hiked the Hazel Creek Trail from Fontana Lake to Welch Ridge Trail to the Appalachian Trail, across Silers Bald to Sams Gap, and down to the Middle Prong of Tremont. Richard Kinter had taken us across Fontana Lake. My husband, William, was to meet us at the end of the Tremont road at 7:00 p.m. He wasn't there. So we walked on down to the Smoky Mountain Institute, where he was waiting. The gate had been closed! It was October 15; we walked 33 miles in all.

Elgin was Elgin Kinter, a hiking companion of Margaret's. Together they founded the Wednesday Hiking Club, which is still hiking every Wednesday. They were also the founders of the 900 Miler Club, whose membership is open only to those who have hiked all 900 miles of trail in the park.

The Wednesday Hiking Club still celebrates Margaret's birthday with a hike to LeConte Lodge atop Mount LeConte.

1934

Helping to Build the Park

Leighton LeHue was more excited than he had ever been in his life. He had just turned seventeen and, even though it was in the midst of the Great Depression, he had just landed a job that would help support his parents. That job had just taken him farther away from home than he had ever been in his life, almost 200 miles. He knew that he would live and work with young men his own age and would have the satisfaction of helping to build a national park.

Leighton was one of several thousand young men, nationwide, who were members of the Civilian Conservation Corps, or CCC. This organization had been created by President Franklin Roosevelt to accomplish two goals: to create jobs during the Depression and to do much-needed conservation work. In Leighton's specific case, he was being sent to help construct facilities in what would come to be called the Great Smoky Mountains National Park.

Getting into the CCC had not been easy, as there were many applicants for each post because the CCC offered good pay. Leighton had been accepted because local officials knew his family was among the poorest of the poor. As a CCC member he would receive free room and board at camp so that his family would not have to provide his food. He also would be paid $25 each month. Of this amount, $20 would be sent directly to his family while he could keep $5.00 as pocket money. These sums of money were substantial by the standards of the day (adults were then paid no more than 15 cents per hour for skilled work, whereas unskilled adults might work all day for 50 cents).

Leighton, like all prospective members, had been required to pass a physical examination to demonstrate that he was free of infectious diseases and was "able to do a reasonable day's work." Most of the young men who failed the physical exam did so because they had the "itch," a skin condition caused by not bathing frequently enough.

So Leighton was justifiably excited and pleased with himself for having met all the requirements for membership in the CCC and for successfully traveling by train to Knoxville, Tennessee, where a car from the CCC camp met him and other new members of the group. As the car drove the young men south, the peaks of the Smoky Mountains rose steadily higher against the horizon.

Registering with the camp authorities was followed by supper in the mess hall, and "lights out" soon followed. The next day brought Leighton an experience he would never forget.

Following a substantial breakfast, Leighton helped load tools into the back of a truck; then he and a dozen more young men climbed into the back of another truck for the ride to their work site. Leaving the CCC camp, which was located near the present-day Sugarlands Visitor Center, the truck followed a winding road through a tunnel of trees alongside a rushing mountain stream. On their left, the sides of Mount LeConte ascended very steeply to a height of a little more than 6,500 feet. It was on this mountain that Leighton was to work.

After a drive that took the wheezing trucks about forty-five minutes, the group reached a spot called Grassy Patch. Here everyone climbed out of the trucks, shouldered picks and shovels, and began to walk up the mountain. A narrow footbridge led across a swift stream, and a few yards farther the trail turned to ascend beside a tributary of the larger stream. Leighton and his coworkers climbed steadily for a mile before taking a rest stop at yet another stream crossing. The stop was at Arch Rock, where the trail crossed the stream they were following and then inched upward between a slab of rock and a sheer cliff face. The top of the slab was propped against the cliff to form a crude arch. After a ten-minute break, Leighton and his crew climbed yet again until they reached their work site.

> All plants and animals in the park are protected. You are the visitor; they live there.

Never had Leighton seen such vegetation. In the hollows along the mountainside, huge hemlocks reached upward 70 feet and more. Tangles of rhododendron were so thick that even animals could not penetrate them. At places where there was no large tree cover and the soil was exposed to direct sunlight, mountain laurel and sand myrtle created a carpet 4 and 5 feet thick. It was the task of Leighton's crew to build a trail through this vegetation, up the side of the steepest mountain east of the Mississippi River.

Despite the cooler air at the high altitude, sweat flowed freely as the CCC trail crews swung axes and shovels. Inch by inch the bushes were hacked back, and shovels leveled the rough surface. After only a few feet of progress, a place was reached where the slope fell away so steeply that no trail could be built on the side of the mountain. The crew  then became human packhorses, carrying or rolling rocks into place to build a ledge on which the trail could run.

Leighton was a wiry youth, accustomed to hard work on the farm, but he was more than ready to eat his lunch when it arrived and then to sprawl on a mossy spot for a rest.

Three more hours of hard work filled the afternoon until the crew left at four o'clock for its hike back down the mountain. All day Leighton had expected to see a bear charge out of the woods or, at the least, to find himself confronting a poisonous snake. The only wildlife he saw, however, was a red squirrel that chattered in disapproval at the trail crew as they passed beneath a large hemlock. Looking back at the place where twelve young men had worked all day, Leighton estimated that seven hours of hard labor had extended the trail by fewer than 40 feet. He ached in every muscle as he dragged his leaden feet back to the truck parked at Grassy Patch.

Leighton LeHue would stay in the Great Smoky Mountains for two years. He would help scrub out the barracks and mess hall every Saturday; he would attend evening classes, which allowed him to finish high school; and he would spend many, many hours on the steep slopes of Mount LeConte. But he would never forget his first day on a CCC trail-building crew.

Author's note: Mr. Leighton LeHue described this event to me in an interview in 1999. At that time, Mr. LeHue was eighty-nine years old. He died in the winter of 2004. The trail he helped build, now called the Alum Cave Bluff Trail, is the most popular trail on Mount LeConte. Two and one-half miles bring a hiker to the sheer cliff of Alum Cave Bluff, whereas 5 miles take one to the top of LeConte and the lodge there. The trailhead for Alum Cave Bluff is on Newfound Gap Road at Grassy Patch. The CCC built hundreds of miles of trails in the park and constructed most of the campgrounds and picnic areas still in use.

1940

A Park at Last

The open car rolled slowly along the steep mountain road, steadily moving upward toward the distant peak. The roadsides were lined with parked cars and curious people who were anxious to catch a glimpse of the large head, the firm jaw, and the cigarette in its long holder clamped at a jaunty angle between the teeth of President Franklin D. Roosevelt.

It was a September day in 1940, near the end of Roosevelt's second term. The president had announced some weeks before that he would seek an unprecedented third term. This surprised few political observers. War had broken out in Europe in September 1939, and the road ahead looked rough for the United States.

Most people felt that Roosevelt had done a fine job fighting the Depression. His various programs to put people to work had kept hunger at bay from a good many mountain homes. That was why so many people in the normally staunch Republican stronghold of East Tennessee were cheering and waving at the Democratic president this day.

"Well," thought Roosevelt to himself, "let us all enjoy ourselves. We may have few chances to do so in the immediate future. This park I am dedicating today will be a place where people can come to enjoy themselves for many years to come. It won't cost much to use the park, either." The legislation establishing the park had labeled it "a pleasuring-ground free to the people."

Smiling and waving to the crowd along the road, President Roosevelt mentally reviewed the history of the park. Local people had first begun talking about the idea of establishing a park around 1920. Even though many people thought the task of creating a park would be impossible, they allowed their names to be used in fund-raising efforts. "I guess they got fooled," Roosevelt chuckled. "We have a park."

In 1926 Congress had authorized the creation of a park but had provided no money for several years. The states of Tennessee and North Carolina had put up money and purchased land from timber companies. Schoolchildren had participated in fund drives. The Rockefeller family had donated $5 million to fund the undertaking. Finally, the park was declared established in 1934, but it had taken another six years to build roads, trails, and other facilities with much of the work being done by the Civilian Conservation Corps, an agency that Roosevelt had created to employ out-of-work young men. On September 2, 1940, the park would be dedicated.

Eleanor Roosevelt nudged the president's elbow and reminded him to pay attention to the road over which they were being driven. They had just reached one of its most interesting points. The ascent here was so steep that the engineers found it necessary to build the road with a full 360-degree turn, corkscrewing upward. Mr. Roosevelt quipped that this was the first time he had met himself coming while still going.

The presidential caravan climbed higher. It had been as warm as summer when they left the Knoxville airport. The temperature was still very much that of summer even in Gatlinburg at the foot of the mountain, but as they climbed the mountain, there was a fall-like freshness in the air. Along the roadside and up the ridges, Roosevelt could see the trees and shrubs of his native New York state. The altitude gain had taken the party into a northern climate zone.

Now people were walking along the road's shoulders, all of them going up the mountain. Many of them were panting, as walking up mountains was not their daily occupation, but they all waved and cheered when the president went by.

Then, ahead, the president saw it—a notch in the highest ridge where the road crossed the crest, State Line Ridge by name, where Tennessee touched North Carolina. There, to his left as the caravan traveled uphill, was a large overlook. The notch was called Newfound Gap, and an elaborate platform constructed of fieldstone marked the site where the dedication ceremonies would be held. This platform, which offered extensive views into both adjoining states, was a memorial to Laura Spelman Rockefeller, the mother of John D. Rockefeller Jr. It was a generous donation from his family, in honor of his mother. This donation was the one that had pushed the acquisition effort for the park over the top.

A cheer went up as the presidential car entered the parking lot. After a flurry of activity by the photographers, the cameras became still. Mr. Roosevelt was being helped from the car into his wheelchair. Out of respect for the president, no one ever took a picture of him receiving physical assistance. Only when he was seated with the other dignitaries did the cameras again click.

> Cherokee Indians do not, and never have, worn feather headdresses or lived in tepees.

Roosevelt looked around him. Crowded up front were the usual lot of state political leaders, anxious to be photographed with the president. Roosevelt did not mind that, but he was not going to rest easy until he shook the hand of one special man. There he was, stuck in the back of the official party. The president motioned to a Secret Service agent. "Go bring that man to me."

Colonel Robert Chapman was not surprised to be at the rear of the platform; he was pleased to even be there at all. "Colonel" was a courtesy title Chapman retained from his days in the National Guard. Chapman was a businessman and civic leader from Knoxville. He had been one of the first to support the idea of a park and had done a great deal of work to make it a reality. Of course, that single-minded dedication to the idea had involved him in controversy. He had fought the timber companies who wanted to hold onto all their land, and he had opposed those who had been ready to settle for a state park or a national forest. Political opponents had forced him off various official boards. One confrontation actually ended in a fistfight. But despite the struggles, today's dedication made it worth it.

"Mr. Chapman, the president would especially like to see you, if that is convenient."

Convenient was not the word Chapman would have chosen—wonderful, marvelous, or outstanding would have been more like it.

"Of course," Chapman replied.

Making his way to the front of the platform, Chapman found Roosevelt had his hand out to shake before he could raise his.

"Mr. President . . . ." he began.

"Bob," Roosevelt interrupted, "this is a grand day for you and for the entire nation. You have a park at last."

Author's note: A large bronze plaque mounted on the stone-viewing platform marks the site where President Roosevelt dedicated the park. The major highway from Knoxville to the park is named the Chapman Highway. Newfound Gap Overlook is the most frequently visited spot in the park. It is located on Newfound Gap Road approximately halfway between the park entrances at Gatlinburg, Tennessee, and Cherokee, North Carolina. Because so much of the land for the park was purchased with private donations, the Great Smoky Mountains National Park is forbidden to charge an entrance fee. This park was not a gift from the government to the people, but it is a bequest from the people to be cared for by their government.

1941

Stubborn Old Women

Even by the standards of the day in the 1940s, a two-room structure with a loft built of squared logs covered by a wood-shingled roof was not much to look at. Heat came from two fireplaces constructed of local stone. Surrounding the humble dwelling were the outbuildings associated with mountain farms: a springhouse, a smokehouse, a barn, and a corncrib. Fields covered a few acres before the surrounding woods and ridges blocked the view.

Not much, but it was their home, and five stubborn old women did not intend to let the government have it. After all, their daddy, "Hairy John" Walker (so-called because of his full beard), had fought for that government in the Civil War. He had been a soldier in the US Artillery when many of his "flatland" neighbors had joined the Confederacy. The sisters felt that they could fight against the government just as well as their daddy had fought for it. The very idea of taking people's homes and farms to make a park was a foreign idea to them, and they were too stubborn to change.

Hettie, Margaret, Louisa, Mary Elizabeth, and Caroline Walker were all stubborn. One had to be to live the way they did. They were a continuation of the lifestyle and attitudes of the nineteenth-century pioneers. Their lives were lived within a small compass of miles in the watershed known as Little Greenbrier, an area not far from Little Greenbrier School, and their days were filled with hard work. They grew corn, which was the basis of their diet and the feed for the animals they raised, but their dinner table was also filled with every variety of vegetable that could be grown in the Smoky Mountains. They ate cherries, peaches, and apples, preserving the apples and peaches for the winter by drying them. Cows provided milk, butter, and cheese; chickens, turkeys, and ducks provided eggs and meat. They seldom ate beef because it was difficult to preserve.

All their clothes were made at home. Winter clothes were made of cloth they wove on a loom their father had made. Only shoes and occasional "special" clothes came from a store, although "Hairy John" even handmade their shoes when he had been alive.

Even when their parents died and Caroline married, life for the other sisters went on much as it always had. Male relatives appeared each spring to help with the heavy work of turning the land and "laying off rows" so that the sisters could plant their crops. The men came again in fall to haul logs from the woods so that firewood could be prepared for winter and for cooking year-round. Yet again, the men came at the first cold spell to help butcher hogs for the winter's meat. Other than these visits from the men, the sisters lived on their own and, except for church services and rare trips to a store in Wear Valley, they saw few people. Even the people of their mountain community considered their way of life rather old-fashioned.

Then, in the 1930s, the talk of a national park penetrated Sisters Cove, the name that had been given to the area where the Walker family lived. Such talk was disturbing to the sisters, because it meant they would have to leave their home and farm and move away. They would be forced to leave behind all the familiar scenes, the memories of a lifetime, and the graves of generations of relatives. So the Walker sisters decided not to leave. They could see no reason for a place where people could play, whereas their days were filled with work.

When community gatherings were held to discuss the park, the Walker sisters stayed home. When letters came inviting them to meet park boosters, the mail was ignored. When neighbors began to talk of their plans to move away, the subject was changed. The sisters had one home, and they intended to stay in it.

One by one, people left the Little Greenbrier section. More and more land was being set aside for the park. In 1939 an official from the Washington office of the Park Service spent several hours with the Walker sisters, trying to convince them to sell or trade their farm. Meeting a stone wall of stubborn opposition, the official urged the sisters to talk over the situation with friends, relatives, and an attorney. The sisters replied that they didn't need to, because no one else knew as much about the place as they did.

The wheels of progress ground slowly, but finely. By 1940 the government of the United States found itself facing the necessity of beginning condemnation proceedings against stubborn old women. Even with the full strength of the national government arrayed against them, the sisters held out. Early in 1941 the sisters made their move. Inviting park officials to their house, they served a dinner featuring the best of their homegrown larder. After dinner, the sisters announced a proposal.

> Someone camps in the Great Smoky Mountains every night of the year.

The Park Service would look pretty bad in the eyes of the public if the newspapers carried stories and pictures of several elderly women being forcibly removed from their homes. The sisters were ready to go that far if necessary, but they were also ready to offer a compromise. If they could stay in their home the rest of their lives, they would sell their farm at a reasonable price.

The park officials were not especially happy with the idea. If a large number of people also wanted to have lifetime occupancy of their property, there would not really be a park but a patchwork of public and private land.

"Take it or leave it," replied the sisters; they were stubborn people and they meant what they said. The Park Service knew when it was beaten. The US government bowed to the will of some stubborn old women.

The last of the sisters left the family home many years later. Margaret died in 1962 at the age of ninety-two, and Louisa lived alone in her mountain home until July 1964. "Hairy John's" house had been vacated by the last of the stubborn old women.

Author's note: You can still visit the Walker sisters' home if you are willing to walk. Park at the Metcalf Bottoms Picnic Area on Little River Road. Cross the road bridge and turn right immediately on the Metcalf Bottoms Trail and continue 0.6 mile to the Little Greenbrier School, constructed of logs in 1882. You can drive to the schoolhouse by using the road, which crosses the river at the picnic grounds, but the walk is nicer. Across the road from the schoolhouse, a gated road goes gently uphill. Follow this road 1 mile to the Walker sisters' home. The walk is 3.2 miles, round-trip, from Metcalf Bottoms Picnic Area.

HARVEY BROOME

[1902–1968]

Harvey Broome was born in Knoxville, Tennessee, only 40 miles north of the Great Smoky Mountains. As a child he spent many weekends on a farm owned by his grandparents, developing a love of the outdoors. When he was fifteen years old his father, George W. Broome, took him on a camping trip to Silers Bald in the Smokies, and a lifelong love affair was born.

After graduation from the University of Tennessee in 1923, Broome enrolled at Harvard, receiving a law degree in 1926. However, his love of the outdoors was so great that he chose to spend most of the rest of his life as a law clerk, since that job gave him more time to be outside.

In 1934 Broome met Benton MacKaye and Bernard Frank at a conference in the Smokies and the three of them formed The Wilderness Society. At the same time Broome was involved in the work of the Great Smoky Mountains Conservation Association, working to create a national park in the Smokies. Writing, speaking, and appearing before various government agencies to advocate for the park took up a great deal of his time.

As the park became a reality Broome clashed with David C. Chapman (see "A Park At Last—1940") over whether the focus of the park should be tourism or wilderness. Broome had the satisfaction of being present in 1964 when President Lyndon Johnson signed the Wilderness Act into law, preserving most of the Smokies as an area where development is prohibited.

Broome was a prolific writer, and three of his books were published following his death: *Faces of the Wilderness*, *Harvey Broome—Earth Man*, and *Under the Skies in the Great Smoky Mountains*. The last book recounts many of his hikes and camping trips in the early days of the park.

1948

Carryin' Momma up the MOUNTAIN

The steep slope of Mount LeConte seemed to stretch up endlessly, much farther than Jack Huff could see. The trail zigged and zagged along contour lines, so much that he had long since lost track of how many turns he had made. From landmarks he knew, however, he had about a mile to go. "One more mile," Jack Huff thought, "one more mile and I can put Momma down."

Jack owned a lodge up the mountain, and it was not strange that he should own one as his family had a tradition of involvement in the hospitality business. In 1918 Andrew Huff, Jack's father, had built the Mountain View Hotel, the first hotel to open in Gatlinburg. Soon people were trickling into the remote little village to enjoy the scenery, the cool mountain air, and the meals that the Huff family spread on the table three times a day.

The most prominent peak in sight of Gatlinburg is Mount LeConte. Although not the highest mountain in the Great Smokies, it is the peak most perpendicular to its base, rising steeply to a height of 6,593 feet. Growing up in the shadow of LeConte, Jack Huff had always been fascinated by the peak. He roamed across its slopes, followed its streams, and scaled its cliffs. He even took his sweetheart there. She loved the mountain, too, so much so that they were married on a summit of LeConte called Myrtle Point.

In 1925 Jack decided to open a lodge atop LeConte. The rugged trail would discourage most visitors, but those who wanted an unusual experience surrounded by wilderness, but with some creature comforts, would come to love the place. By 1936 LeConte Lodge had become much what it is at present—a central reception cabin, a kitchen and dining hall, and several small cabins for sleeping. Mule trains brought in supplies, and there were pit toilets.

> One of the loudest animal noises in the park is made by one of the smallest animals, the red squirrel.

Jack's mother heard praise about the lodge from those who began their visit at the Mountain View in Gatlinburg and then climbed LeConte for a day or two at Jack's lodge. Although his mother, in times past, had walked a lot in and over the mountains, she was growing frail, and he knew she could not walk up LeConte to visit his lodge. The mule train was not an option, either, because the uneven trail made any ride up the mountain quite rough. Although she never talked about her wish to see Jack's mountaintop lodge, her eager conversation with visitors who had been there and her longing looks at the peak gave away her thoughts.

Equally quietly, Jack began to experiment. He took an old kitchen chair and some leather straps. He padded the chair where it would rest on his back, and he altered the legs so that they would not inhibit his stride. After some preliminary tests, he got his mother to try out the perch. More adjustments were called for, and in April, when the wildflowers were at their peak, Jack was ready. His mother weighed ninety-eight pounds, a good load to carry even for a mountain man. Jack had walked the trail to the top of LeConte many times but never with a load quite like this one. Jack was carrying his "Momma" up the mountain.

The trail up the mountain followed the banks of Mill Creek (now called LeConte Creek), so named because fourteen mills had been located on it before the national park was established.

Even at the beginning of their trek, the trail was steep, so Mrs. Huff took her seat in the chair and Jack hoisted her on his back. Up the creek they went, passing out of the orchard area and on past the house site once occupied by Indian Bill, a noted herb doctor and the last Cherokee to live in the Gatlinburg area. As they made their way up the trail and entered the unbroken forest, rhododendron, galax, mountain laurel, arbutus, and patches of pink lady slipper surrounded them.

The air was cool, but Jack was sweating before they reached Rainbow Falls, a prominent landmark on their trail. An older trail had gone up almost beside the falls, but they chose a trail built by the Civilian Conservation Corps, which took Jack and his mother out Rocky Spur for a view of LeConte Creek valley on one side and Roaring Fork Creek on the other. Moving on above the falls, the Huffs encountered a vista that included a view of the streets of Gatlinburg far below.

The trail reached 4,800 feet at Rocky Spur, but it continued its unrelenting ascent. Not too much farther was the summit near Myrtle Point, where Jack and his wife had been married. At a little more than 6 miles from their starting place, Jack reached the intersection with Bullhead Trail. At this point, the crest was level enough for his mother to walk the rest of the way, and Jack gave a quiet sigh of relief as he put down the chair.

Mrs. Huff was truly pleased when she saw the lodge. She saw the buildings of weathered wood and the inviting porches with their rustic but comfortable chairs, and she smelled the tantalizing aroma carried by the smoke from the kitchen chimney. She was proud of what her son had done with his lodge, and she was proud of him for carrying his Momma up the mountain.

Author's note: Because LeConte Lodge predated the park, it was "grandfathered" into the park plans, whereas almost all other developments were ruled out. Today the lodge is the only overnight facility in the park other than camping shelters. In the 1980s ecological concerns prompted a plan to close the lodge, but a public outcry caused that plan to be abandoned. The lodge is perhaps the best-loved place in the park among travelers who visit the Smokies regularly. Because of its popularity, reservations for overnight stays need to be made months in advance. Now there are no more mule trains. Helicopters carry heavy supplies to the lodge two or three times a year, and a train of llamas, whose padded hoofs are easier on the trails than the hoofs of mules, bring other supplies on a weekly basis. There are several trails up Mount LeConte, all steep. The most popular is the Alum Cave Bluff Trail. The trailhead is on Newfound Gap Road between Gatlinburg and Cherokee.

1950

Unto These Hills

July 1, 1950, was a day that had been long awaited by Harry Buchanan and the other members of the Cherokee Historical Association (CHA). It was a day that would forever change Cherokee, North Carolina, and the Qualla Boundary Reservation of the Eastern Band of the Cherokee Indians. Since March 1948 the association had been working to create an outdoor drama that would depict "the history, both legendary and factual, of the Cherokee Indians . . . in western North Carolina and the area immediately adjacent thereto." Other groups had tried to accomplish this goal and had failed, so the Cherokee Historical Association was worried about meeting the challenge.

Things needed to change in the Cherokee area. The national park had brought some prosperity to the mountains, but very little of it had come to the North Carolina side. Jobs were scarce, and the economy of the town was stagnant. On July 1, 1950, the town of Cherokee had only one telephone and that was in the office of the Bureau of Indian Affairs. The town had no traffic lights, no police department, and almost no tourists. The local economy depended on subsistence farming and whatever aid might come to the Cherokee from the Bureau of Indian Affairs. The CHA, when it began the project of producing the drama, had no theater, no script, no producer, and no director. All it had was a dream, the dream of an outdoor drama that would draw a flood of people with money to spend to the area.

One of the most nervous people in Cherokee on July 1 was Kermit Hunter. Although he was a seasoned script-writer and dramatist, this project had seemed to drag on and on until its deadline had arrived and still there were unanswered questions. Several details about Cherokee history were especially elusive, and the closest reference library was hours away via a winding mountain highway. The script had received a title only a few weeks before. Though several titles had been considered while the script was still being written and rehearsals were in progress, a phrase from Psalms had finally been selected as the title because it best described the strength the drama was to portray: *Unto These Hills*.

Hunter was confident that the setting of the drama and its subject made his choice of themes appropriate. The drama would include the tragedy of the removal of the Cherokee people from Cherokee values of their homeland and their subsequent exile to Oklahoma. Hunter had chosen also to emphasize their cooperation and sense of justice.

Hunter was nervous that the general public would not understand the centrality of these themes to the

Cherokee experience. After all, the performers were not feather-wearing, tepee-dwelling, tomahawk-wielding Indians of Hollywood creation. They were Indians wearing only an occasional feather and a turban on their heads and living in well-constructed permanent houses. Although this was not the image the public had in mind, it was an accurate depiction of the Cherokee. The performance was to be the real story of the real people.

On opening day the final touches had to be put on the Woodland Theater, an amphitheater sculpted out of a Smoky Mountain hill by local labor, some of it volunteer. A budget of $65,000 had been established, but only $35,000 had been raised by July 1. The not-yet-open production was already deeply in debt.

General manager Carol White was nervously looking at the end of a list of chores that still needed to be finished. Margie Douthit was also nervous. Although she was not performing, she worked in the office and felt an attachment to the drama—as if she had found her true home. She developed a sense of belonging in Cherokee.

In the backstage area more than 350 authentic costumes were ready, moves and cues were all committed to memory, and dances had been rehearsed until they could be executed flawlessly. Two-thousand-plus seats were ready in Woodland Theater, and tickets had been sold. No one was worried about remembering lines, because the dialogue was read by a narrator who spoke to the audience over a sound system.

Another matter nervously watched was the weather. The Smoky Mountains are the rainiest place in eastern North America. During the day the heat and humidity gather in the valleys and are then sucked up to form clouds over the peaks; by late afternoon there is a cloudburst somewhere in the mountains. The theater company knew the threat of rain would be as effective as an actual storm in keeping the audience away.

Fortunately, on opening day, the sun neared the western hills that rose against a blue, cloudless sky. The performers had on their makeup and costumes, the preshow music began, and the crowds began to stream in. Over the next two and a half hours, *Unto These Hills* portrayed in fourteen scenes the history of the Cherokee people from the time of the Spanish explorer Hernando de Soto in the sixteenth century until the death of the great Cherokee chief Junaluska in 1842. The music, the dance, and the narration satisfied the audience, and there was a spontaneous standing ovation when the lights dimmed for the last time. Only then did the tense nerves of the writer, director, performers, and local citizens relax.

July 1, 1950, was a turning point in the life of the town of Cherokee, North Carolina, and in the existence of the Eastern Band of the Cherokee Indians. None of the fifty-three performances in the first season were canceled because of rain, and a total of 107,140 people attended. The entire debt acquired to produce the drama was paid in the first month, and money was banked for the future. By the end of the 2002 season, almost six million people had seen performances of *Unto These Hills* since its opening day, with many people attending repeat performances year after year. The effect of that July 1950 performance has not been confined to the theater. Drama schools and workshops have been held in the local community in order to increase the number of roles and opportunities available for Cherokee actors. In 1989 James Bradley became the first Qualla Cherokee to star in the Eagle Dance as the Lead Eagle.

In 1952 Oconaluftee Indian Village opened adjacent to the Woodland Theater. This reconstruction of an eighteenth-century Cherokee village shows village life as it existed before contact with Europeans, and it gives the Cherokee a place to demonstrate traditional crafts such as beadwork and pottery making. In continuing the development of demonstrations  of Cherokee culture, the Cherokee Botanical Garden and Nature Trail opened in 1954. The Museum of the Cherokee Indian has belonged to the CHA since 1952. In 1976 it moved into a striking building that houses the "greatest collection of Cherokee artifacts in existence." More recently the museum has been renovated to incorporate holograms and walk-through exhibits.

Unto These Hills has brought millions of people and hundreds of millions of dollars to Cherokee, North Carolina, since July 1, 1950. Its greatest accomplishment cannot be measured in dollars or in the other businesses it has stimulated. Through stirring pride in the traditional ways, this drama has preserved the crafts and the history of the Eastern Band of the Cherokee people.

Author's note: The Qualla Craft Shop, Museum of the Cherokee Indian, Oconaluftee Village, and Woodland Theater are located adjacent to US Route 441, also named Newfound Gap Road, the transmountain highway that crosses the Great Smoky Mountains National Park. Performances of the drama are held Monday through Saturday from June to August. The Qualla Craft Shop sells crafts made on the Qualla Boundary Reservation by members of the Eastern Band of the Cherokee. Margie Douthit, who was present on opening day, worked with the drama for more than fifty years and later became the marketing director of the CHA. She had, indeed, found a home.

1957

The Walking
Mountain Preacher

The stereotypical image of a mountain preacher conjures up images of a tall, thin, white-haired man with a gleam in his eye as he hurries from one small congregation to another. Because he is often walking, we probably picture him with a staff in his hand, rather like Moses leading the Children of Israel. Popular stereotypes also suggest that the preacher is not well educated, perhaps only barely literate.

Outwardly, Rufus Morgan fit the stereotype—his clerical collar was likely to be worn under a flannel hiking shirt. But the fact was that he was an Episcopal priest whose proper title was the Reverend Dr. Rufus Morgan.

Rufus had been serving churches in western North Carolina for twenty years, often serving as pastor for as many as eleven churches at once and driving as much as 40,000 miles a year to reach them all on a regular basis. All of this work was not an easy task for a man his age, but he was also a man of great faith. He was confident that his God would provide what was needed in order to accomplish his work. Once Rufus was asked for advice about paying off a church debt. He said, "I am your spiritual leader and I believe that if we take care of the spiritual part, the money part will take care of itself." As it happens, it did.

One special day in October, the bright, blue sky and the vivid colors of the autumn leaves alone would have made this a day to remember, but there were two other factors on Rufus Morgan's mind. It was his seventy-second birthday, and, as he did every year, he was celebrating by climbing Mount LeConte. In addition, he was celebrating his retirement, sort of a retirement, at least. Instead of serving eleven parishes, he would cut back to one, plus occasional services at others. In addition to continuing some church duties, he would work on maintaining 50-plus miles of the Appalachian Trail and promoting other conservation causes.

As he made his way up the Alum Cave Bluff Trail that October day, Rufus had a lot to think about. The peaks of the surrounding mountains were reminders of his ancestors on his mother's side, who had come to the area before the Cherokee departed. Off to the west he would be able to see Silers Bald, named for his predecessors, Albert and Joanna Siler.

Along the trail Rufus not only felt one with his personal past, he felt one with his creator. He felt that walking in the mountains was a good time and place to worship the creator of the timeless hills. As he was fond of telling people, the word saunter was derived from Old French san terre, meaning "holy earth," and that was exactly what he felt the earth to be, holy.

Although he lived less than 75 miles from the renowned gardens of the Biltmore Estate owned by the Vanderbilt family, Rufus had never bothered to visit the gardens. He knew the gardens were beautiful, but he also knew they were man-made. His idea of beauty revolved around rhododendron, mountain laurel, and wildflowers that grew naturally in the mountains. The Vanderbilt forest reserve on Mount Pisgah was for him, not the formal gardens at the estate.

Not surprisingly, Rufus's favorite hero, outside of the pages of the Bible, was Saint Francis of Assisi, the venerable saint who had preached to the birds and woodland creatures and who had dedicated himself to bringing peace. "I've tried to live by that," Rufus thought as he trod steadily up the trail.

As he climbed up LeConte, the view opened up to the south and west. "Over there," he thought, "behind the peak of Clingman's Dome, is where my life began in Franklin, North Carolina." Near there he had deceived his bishop, something every good priest has to do now and then. His family had lived on Cartoogechaye Creek and had worshipped in St. John's church. That church had been abandoned as the congregation dwindled in size until eventually the building was torn down in 1925. Rufus wanted to see that church rebuilt, so he began to do the work with his own hands and his own money. Slowly, a beautifully handcrafted building arose, each stage done carefully and painstakingly, each phase paid for before the next began. When the building was finished, the bishop was called to consecrate a church he didn't even know he had. It was quite a joke, Rufus remembered, to see the look of relief on the bishop's face when he was told the gem of a building was debt free.

He was nearing the top now. He reflected for a moment on how he missed hiking with his sister, Lucy. She had been active in helping found the Penland School of Crafts and the Southern Highland Handicraft Guild. For several years he had been the chaplain of the Penland School she founded, and so he saw his sister nearly every day. Now he missed her company. But, he mused, both of us live on in the students we taught there, and he was satisfied. Penland had been virgin territory for the Episcopal Church when he went there. The Episcopal Church was not one of the traditional denominations of the mountain people. People of the mountains saw the church as a meager charity, providing old clothes and not much else. Rufus wanted the church to do more: He wanted to provide the dignity of earning a living through useful work. The most readily available work was relearning the old-time crafts, and that had become his goal and that of his sister. It was a great satisfaction to him to know that the craft tradition was now firmly reestablished in the Smoky Mountains.

> In the Smoky Mountains, a "bald" is not a person with no hair; it is a treeless mountaintop.

Rufus was at the top now. The trail turned to the right and leveled out. It wasn't far now to LeConte Lodge. But before going there, the priest took a detour to his right and shortly came out on the edge of the bluff. Before him, wave after wave, rolled the Smoky Mountains, the land he loved and would always call home. There he remembered a wedding. A couple from the University of Pennsylvania had called and asked him to perform their wedding ceremony atop LeConte. In keeping with the tradition of the bride and groom not seeing each other before the ceremony, one group hiked Trillium Gap Trail and the other Alum Cave Bluff Trail. At sunset the group walked out to Cliff Top to watch the colors in the sky, and the wedding was performed in the open air. The "reception" was a cake baked by the kitchen staff at LeConte Lodge.

"A wonderful day, and climbing LeConte has been a wonderful way to celebrate," he thought, "but retire? Only officially. There is too much work yet to do to stop now. I'll just keep going one step at a time."

Author's note: Dr. Rufus Morgan climbed LeConte for the last time on his ninety-second birthday, having ascended the mountain at least 175 times. He died in 1983 at the age of ninety-eight and is buried near Franklin in St. John's Cartoogechaye Episcopal Church Cemetery. The memory of the Walking Mountain Preacher is honored by the Rufus Morgan Trail, which leads to Rufus Morgan Falls.

JUNALUSKA
[TSUNU'LAHUN'SKI]

[C. 1775–1868]

Junaluska, a leader of the Cherokee people from the War of 1812 until after their removal to Oklahoma, was born about 1775 near the southwest border of the Great Smoky Mountains National Park. As he grew up, his homeland was coming under the pressure of settlement from white settlers flooding across the Appalachian Mountains. Junaluska opposed this settlement but could not find an effective way of ending it.

When the War of 1812 began, the government of the United States claimed the British were inciting the Native American tribes along the frontier to attack the white settlers. Andrew Jackson, among others, appealed to long-standing hostilities between the Native American tribes and convinced Junaluska, and other Cherokee, to join US forces in attacking the Cherokee's traditional enemy, the Creeks.

At the battle of Horseshoe Bend Junaluska swam across the Tallapoosa River and brought several canoes belonging to the Creek fighters. He then used these canoes to ferry his followers across and attack the Creeks from the rear. This attack allowed the US forces to attack successfully from the front of the Creek position. During the fighting, much of it hand to hand, Junaluska is said to have saved the life of Andrew Jackson, who was being attacked by two Creek fighters. As a reward for his service Junaluska was given 640 acres of land near his original home. He lived there for several years with his wife and three children.

Despite being a hero of the battle of Horseshoe Bend, and a veteran of armed service to the United States, Junaluska was forced from his home during the "Trail of Tears" and settled in what is today Oklahoma. In 1847 he returned to his Smoky Mountain home and was allowed to stay. He died at Robbinsville, North Carolina, on October 20, 1868, and is buried there.

1985

Bridal Shower

Ramona Shelton knew everyone in the room, even though the fellowship hall of the rural Baptist church near Newport, Tennessee, was quite full. Not only did she know all the people there, she was related to almost all of them. In just three weeks Ramona was going to be married, and all these people had come to celebrate with her by attending a bridal shower in her honor. There was one puzzling thing: There was only one gift on the table in the center of the room. True, the box wrapped in paper with a bridal motif was large, but just one gift was unusual. On these occasions the hostesses usually would go together to get a gift, but the other guests brought their individual presents. This time it looked as if everyone invited had pooled his or her resources for one gift.

Well, the gifts didn't really matter. In three weeks she would be Ramona Hall, and being with Jack was all she really wanted. Gifts were nice mementos from friends and family, but Ramona was not mercenary. The good times she would have at the party were important to her, but the years ahead were the real focus. Still, she did wonder what was in that big box. And she did wonder if she and Jack would be able to continue living in the mountains. So many people her age had been forced to leave the hills to find jobs in the cities, and all of them she knew said they missed their mountain homes even though they enjoyed the money and convenience city living brought with it. Like most of the mountain people, Ramona had a strong attachment to the land and did not want to give up living in the place she loved.

Ramona could have traced her family tree back four generations by just looking around the room. Her two sisters and her two sisters-in-law were present; so were her mother with her three sisters as well as two aunts-in-law. Her grandmother and her two surviving sisters were there, flitting around the hall trying to talk to everybody at once. The person to whom Ramona's eye kept returning to was her great-grandmother, Momma Essie. She was ninety-one years old.

"How much life in these mountains has changed since Momma Essie was a bride," Ramona thought. "I wish I knew and could remember the story of each of my relatives here today. They have quite a story to tell. Especially Essie." Little did Ramona know that her wish would soon be fulfilled.

Momma Essie let the party flow over her like a mountain stream going over a rock. Her blue eyes sparkled in her wrinkled face; her mind was alert to all that was going on around her, but she was bothered a little by the noisy talk. With so many people talking at once, she could hear only individual words when people talked to her; otherwise, she could not make out the conversation. But despite the noise, Momma Essie was having a very good time. She knew what was in the big, gaily wrapped box.

The guests all found chairs around the walls of the hall, and they played some games, silly games, but they were fun. They had a contest to see which group could best dress up as a "bride," using tissue paper for a headdress and veil. They played guessing games about the contents of a box, with hints implying that it was something Ramona and Jack would need in private, intimate ways—the box held two new toothbrushes. The older relatives told stories about Ramona as a little girl. And then, finally, it was time to open the gift.

Ramona was escorted to the table where the large box rested, and she was asked to sit. Another chair was placed opposite her, and Momma Essie was escorted to the seat of honor.

"Now, Ramona, honey," Momma Essie began, "you can unwrap that box in just a minute. But here's what all of us has done. We hope you and Jack can stay and live here in sight of the Smoky Mountains, but, being young and all, it may be y'all has to leave to find work. Anyways, some of us old ones won't be here much longer to know what all you may do. So all of us kinfolks has done fixed you a gift to always remind you of who you are and where you come from. Now open your present."

Hands trembling and with tears in her eyes, Ramona unwrapped the box. It held a handmade quilt large enough for a king-size bed. Each quilt square was embroidered with hundreds of tiny stitches that represented a scene from Ramona's life or from her family history. Each square was also embroidered with the name of the person who made the square. Momma Essie said, "Back in 1911, when I got married, my momma give me a quilt. That square right in the middle is the one I made for you. That's a picture of the ole cabin my momma and daddy lived in and where I was raised. The Park taken the old place, and the house is no more. That next square represents the church where lots of our folks is buried. We go back there for Decoration Day every May, and you have been there many a time, Ramona. Look, here is the square your grandma done. It shows a old-timey pump like the one we had when she was a girl. That square there showing a bridal bouquet of flowers is the one your own momma done. There is six dozen of these squares, each one telling something different about you and your family, and each square is done by a different family member. The border around the whole quilt is green and blue to remind you of these hills and the sky above them. All your kinfolks come to my room this last summer, few at a time, and we sewed this here quilt for you, using the very same quilting frame my husband made for me not long after we was married. Now, be careful, baby girl, what you dream the first night you and Jack sleeps under this quilt. The first dream dreamed under a new quilt always comes true."

"Butt" refers, in the Smoky Mountains, to the abrupt end of a mountain ridge.

Ramona did not know what she might dream about, but she was sure that she would never forget who she was or where she came from. Her bridal-shower gift would always remind her of those things.

One of the outstanding characteristics of the Appalachian people is their attachment to place. Ramona was true to her roots in not wanting to leave the mountains and in carrying memories of them if she did leave.

Author's note: The craft of quilt making is an old one in the Appalachian Mountains. Quilt tops are "pieced" together, sometimes from blocks of material, but traditionally the piecing is done with small scraps of cloth. This tradition dates back to the time when cloth was woven by hand from thread spun at home. Even the smallest piece of cloth represented many hours of labor.

1993

Being Prepared Saved Lives

Marcy Paisley had not seen this much snow all winter. She had spent the entire season at her home in Detroit, and not once, all winter, had there been this much snow. The white stuff came up to her knees; the drifts were 4 feet deep. Marcy was in a remote part of the Great Smoky Mountains National Park, but she was not alone. She was part of a group of 117 students and faculty from the Cranbrook/Kingswood Upper Schools in Bloomfield Hills, a Detroit suburb. The group had traveled to the park as part of an annual event, which was based on the concepts developed by the Outward Bound program.

Since 1971 Cranbrook had sponsored a ten-day camping and hiking event in the Great Smoky Mountains for some of its students. The group would arrive at the park by bus and break into small groups of fewer than a dozen students, with each group led by faculty members and senior students. The outing included such activities as hiking 6 miles a day, cooking meals on camp stoves, building campfires, and practicing outdoors skills. Such activities were designed to build self-confidence, self-esteem, and group cohesion. Participation in the event had become something of a rite of passage for the sophomore class members.

Cranbrook School leaders made careful preparations for the trip. Each participant underwent seven weeks of physical conditioning so that the steep climbs would not be exhausting. Each person completed a two-hour course on how to avoid hypothermia, a potentially fatal condition brought on by getting wet without the opportunity to dry off. Wet clothing and wet skin can rapidly lower the body temperature to the point that death occurs. Hypothermia can set in at temperatures as high as 50 degrees Fahrenheit. In addition, each participant was to be properly equipped with a waterproof/windproof coat, good boots, and a sleeping bag, and each group carried food for ten days along with stoves and fuel. These careful preparations and a cautious attitude would save many lives in just a few days.

A happy, excited group of students and faculty boarded buses in Detroit on March 6 for the trip to the Smoky Mountains. As the group traveled south, it seemed they were running into the very arms of spring. After the harsh Michigan winter, the temperature in Tennessee seemed almost balmy. Even when the group arrived in the mountains and checked in with the rangers on the North Carolina side of the park, the cool evenings did not seem much of a weather challenge.

Park officials, however, were concerned about the long-range forecast. Although predicting the weather a week in advance cannot be done with a great deal of accuracy, there were warnings about the possibility of a storm. The rangers knew the heaviest snow often comes to the park in spring, so they advised the Cranbrook group to keep an eye on the weather and to carry out as much of their program as possible at lower altitudes.

As the small groups of students and faculty entered the woods, they saw the signs of the coming spring. Leaf buds were swollen, the ferns were poking "fiddleheads" up through the detritus of leaves, birdsong filled the air, and the sun felt warm on the students' shoulders.

The first days of the trip went as planned. Each group camped at a separate backcountry site and carried out their planned activities, working on developing outdoor and camping skills, enjoying nature, and bonding as a group. As days passed and the weather seemed good, some of the groups moved higher up the mountains.

On Friday night, March 12, 1993, the Cranbrook School campers were spread over a wide area of the park, just as they had planned. They were approaching the end of their stay with only a few days left. That night, as the groups slept, the Blizzard of '93 struck. This massive storm brought bad weather from Key West to Nova Scotia, causing more than $800 million in damages.

The dramatic change in their conditions startled some of the students. One of them later said the scariest time of all was waking up to find 3 feet of snow on her tarpaulin shelter. Some of the groups recognized the futility of attempting to move and simply sat down to wait for a thaw. These groups were wise, but boredom made waiting difficult, and the uncertainty of their situation gnawed at their confidence.

Other groups began to move down the slopes and immediately experienced difficulty. Any movement in the deep snow was difficult. Obstacles were hidden by the white blanket until the hiker stumbled over them, and stream crossings often meant wet feet as stepping-stones and foot logs were coated with ice. Such conditions also made it difficult to cook. Soon those groups trying to hike were tired, and some signs of hypothermia and frostbite were becoming apparent.

> Smoky Mountain pioneers did not wear "leather britches"; they ate them. Leather britches was the name for beans dried in the pod and then boiled, hull and all.

Back in Detroit there was growing anxiety among parents and relatives of the campers. The students stranded in the mountains had not carried cell phones or walkie-talkies, because the rugged terrain makes communicating with such devices difficult.

One group, accompanied by Marcy Paisley and Mark Penske, seemed to be at the limits of its physical ability. Several of the students felt they could go no farther, so a camp was made for the night. After all the students were settled in, Marcy and Mark set out to find help. They struggled through the woods for 3 miles and had gotten wet to the waist when they smelled smoke. Soon they were at the camp of some fishermen who dried them out, fed them, and told them hundreds of National Guardsmen and park rangers were looking for them.

The park authorities had reacted swiftly when the storm struck. As soon as the heavy snowfall lifted on Saturday, rangers began trying to follow the trails, some on foot and some on all-terrain vehicles, to find stranded hikers. The Tennessee and North Carolina National Guard were contacted for help. When the winds subsided enough to allow flight, army  helicopters entered the search, some of the copters being provided by the 101st Airborne Division from Fort Campbell, Kentucky. On Monday hikers began to be brought out of the mountains. By Tuesday only twenty-four of the Cranbrook School group were unaccounted for. One group never even knew anyone was in trouble. That group completed its scheduled hike, finished its programs, and walked out of the woods precisely at the time and place expected. Still, there was anxiety for the remaining twenty-four campers.

At 1:30 p.m. on Tuesday, March 16, Chief Warrant Officer Glenn Kluttz was flying his National Guard helicopter over one of the trails, looking for the final missing group. Kluttz popped over a ridge in the Hazel Creek area of the park, near Fontana Lake, and the remaining students were standing in the trail below, waving at him.

Naturally, some of the stranded students had been worried, even afraid at times. There had been trying moments and stiff physical challenges to meet. But good planning and careful preparation before setting out, along with a cautious approach to the mountains, brought all 117 students and faculty home safely. Preparation saved lives.

2000

You Can Take the Girl Out of the Mountains

Representatives of some of the most prestigious publishing firms in America began to applaud, then they stood, and then they cheered as a beautiful middle-aged woman with golden hair made her way to the podium. This sophisticated audience of intellectual commerce was honoring a woman who had begun life as one of twelve children in a small cabin in Sevier County, Tennessee.

Country music and movie fans all over the world would be able to recognize her at first glance. The country music fans might well have expected to see her dressed in a flashy costume with a flowing "big hair" wig. Movie buffs might have expected someone who usually portrayed a narrowly defined role, a secretary from *Nine to Five* or a hairdresser in *Steel Magnolias*. But those who knew the real Dolly would not have been surprised at the grace with which she wore her designer gown that night, nor would they have hesitated to talk about the alert intellect and astute business sense that lurked beneath the wigs and makeup. But she was not being honored for her talent as a musician or an actress this time, although numerous honors for both these talents had come her way. Dolly Parton was receiving the award called "Honors" from the American Association of Publishers. She won the award because of her philanthropy and a community-service program sponsored by her Dollywood Foundation, a program called Imagination Library.

Dolly Rebecca Parton was the fourth of twelve children born to Robert Lee and Avie Parton. Although the family worked hard on their hilly farm, their financial circumstances could almost have served as a stereotype of Appalachian poverty. Also stereotypical of Appalachia was their pride, their desire to be self-sufficient, and their attachment to the land and to one another.

Dolly left her native Sevier County, in the shadows of the Great Smoky Mountains, the day after her high-school graduation to go to the country music mecca of Nashville, some 200 miles to the west. She had been singing on local radio shows—and anywhere else opportunities arose—and had written songs ever since she was seven years old. She went to Nashville with superb self-confidence. She felt that with hard work and determination, she could become a star.

The Park Service makes molasses from sorghum cane in the old manner in Cades Cove each October.

She had some success in the music-recording industry, but her big break came in 1967, when one of the superstars of that day, Porter Wagoner, asked her to appear regularly on his syndicated television program. National exposure to a weekly audience of forty-five million people brought national acclaim and celebrity status to Dolly. Awards, recognition, record and movie contracts, and money all came her way. Over the years Dolly was named the Country Music Association's "Female Vocalist of the Year" twice, was picked as "Entertainer of the Year," won four Grammys for her records, twenty-two of which would reach the number-one position on the country or pop charts, and won Golden Globe and People's Choice nominations for roles in two of her movies. But even as her name became a household word, Dolly's heart kept turning back to her native Tennessee Smoky Mountains. Indeed, her heart never left there.

In Sevier County jobs were hard to come by. Over a third of high-school students dropped out before graduation. Dolly wondered how much talent and how many lives were buried under the poverty of the beautiful mountains. She loved the mountains and wanted to preserve some of the old ways, which she felt embodied virtues and values. But some of the old ways included lack of opportunity and poverty—this needed to be changed. Dolly knew that with her celebrity status she could be a role model, demonstrating how to make the most out of what you have. She wanted to pass along to her Smoky Mountain neighbors the skill of making the most out of what you have.

As a first step in addressing the problems of her home county, Dolly purchased a local amusement park, Silver Dollar City, and transformed it into Dollywood. Instead of a generic amusement park that portrayed a generic frontier town, Dollywood became a showcase for talented young entertainers as well as a source of employment for the mountain people. Although a start, this was not enough to satisfy Dolly's desire to give back to her beloved mountain community.

In 1988 Dolly founded the not-for-profit Dollywood Foundation to allow her to give back even more. The initial program of the foundation was to encourage seventh- and eighth-grade students in Sevier County to choose "Buddies," who would encourage each other to stay in school. Upon graduation each "Buddy" would receive a $500 college scholarship. By 1993 the program had reduced the high-school dropout rate from 35 percent to 14.6 percent.

Reading, Dolly thought, was a key to lifelong success. In November 1995 Imagination Library was introduced to help children achieve this end. Dolly has said that it was intended to "help children dream more, learn more, care more, and be more." The ambitious goal of the program was to expand Imagination Library across the United States and then across the world. As part of Imagination Library, when a child is born in Sevier County, the parents are given a hardback copy of *The Little Engine That Could* and a registration card. After registering, that child receives an age-appropriate book each month through age five. The program also gives each child an expandable bookcase for their library, one end of which is shaped like a railroad engine and the other end like a caboose.

On the day she received the American Association of Publishers award, Dolly's program had distributed more than 200,000 books. As she walked to the podium to receive the award, the master of ceremonies reminded the audience that the award was given to "those outside the publishing field who have helped focus public attention on American books and their importance in our society." But Dolly was thinking, "You can take the girl out of the mountains, but you can't take the mountains out of the girl."

Author's note: The Dollywood Foundation has raised more than $4 million for Imagination Library, and the program has spread to Kansas, Georgia, South Carolina, and Alabama. In addition to distributing books, the foundation awards nine college scholarships in Sevier County high schools. Years ago Dolly Parton asked her fan club to disband so that the members' support would be directed to the foundation and not to herself. Dollywood theme park is the premier amusement park in the vicinity of the Great Smoky Mountains. It is located north of the Great Smoky Mountains National Park in the town of Pigeon Forge. The park features rides, musical shows, and traditional crafts and offers a variety of dining experiences.

BENTON MACKAYE

[1879–1975]

Perhaps the most iconic image of the Great Smoky Mountains is that of a hiker with a large pack on his back walking along the most iconic of all Smoky Mountain tracks, the Appalachian Trail. This long-distance trail, stretching from Georgia to Maine, owes its existence to Benton MacKaye.

MacKaye was a high-school dropout who managed to enroll at Harvard, teach on the faculty there in the School of Forestry, work for several government agencies, including the Tennessee Valley Authority, and become the author of numerous articles on regional planning and on conservation. It was MacKaye's work with the Tennessee Valley Authority that brought him to Knoxville and began his involvement with the Smoky Mountains.

A lifelong nature lover, MacKaye spent as much time outdoors as he could and felt that contact with nature was a source of knowledge. Shortly after the death of his wife in 1921 he wrote an article that appeared in the *Journal of the Institute of Architecture*.

In this article, "An Appalachian Trail: A Project in Regional Planning," MacKaye proposed the creation of a trail following the crest of the Appalachian Mountains, and encouraged people to dedicate one week a year to the development of that trail. He suggested that this resource would afford American workers with opportunities for recreation, study, and recuperation from the unhealthy effects of living in large industrial cities.

By 1923 the first section of the Appalachian Trail had been built. By 1936 the trail ran from Maine to Georgia, and the first through hike was made in 1948 by Earl Shaffer. In 1968 MacKaye had the satisfaction of seeing Congress pass a law that created the National Trails System, protecting the Appalachian Trail from commercial development.

Today a separate trail named for Benton MacKaye traverses the mountains from Springer Mountain, Georgia, to the Great Smoky Mountains, where it intersects with the Appalachian Trail.

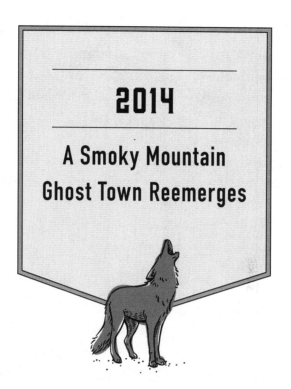

2014

A Smoky Mountain Ghost Town Reemerges

In October 2014 *Huffington Post* carried an article in which a visitor to the Great Smoky Mountains National Park told of discovering a "ghost town" in the park. The story went viral on social media as readers assumed a long-lost, totally forgotten group of ruins had been discovered. The entire event was based on a misinterpretation of what the writer of the article meant. The writer had "discovered" a collection of abandoned houses as something new to him, as "I just discovered a new restaurant." The houses made famous in 2014 were well known and had been for well over a century. Nonetheless, the structures have an interesting story to tell.

In 1901 Colonel Wilson B. Townsend purchased 86,000 acres of land along Little River so he could cut the timber growing there. A railroad was built into the area to haul the logs out to the sawmill constructed by Townsend's company and to take the sawed lumber to market. As the trees suitable for lumber were cut the land was sold to families, mostly from Knoxville, who wanted a second home where they could escape the summer heat. The railway that took lumber out was soon bringing in temporary residents. The families building summer cottages formed an association called the "Appalachian Club," a private organization. Since many of the men were members of the Elks Club, they chose to call their new community Elkmont. They built a clubhouse to serve as a social center for the residents.

Although the numbers of people wishing to join the Appalachian Club were growing, memberships were limited, so a second association was formed, called the Wonderland Club. The Wonderland Park Hotel had been constructed in 1912, and the new group purchased this building and closed it to the general public so it could become a residential site for their members. Some of the Wonderland Club members chose to construct their own cottages in the vicinity of the hotel. Soon informal neighborhoods existed along Little River, Daisy Town, Millionaire's Row, and Society Hill. With two flourishing groups flocking to Elkmont in the summer, their colony became the second-largest town in the county—at least, during the warm months.

Some families living in the vicinity of Elkmont traced their history on the land to the early nineteenth century. Jacob Hauser had settled along Jakes Creek about 1840, giving his name to one of the streams in the area. David Owenby moved to the same area soon after. Levi Trentham built a cabin along Jakes Creek about 1830. These families found the summer residents a positive addition to the local economy. They sold milk, butter, garden vegetables, honey, and firewood to the temporary residents, and some young women found jobs as cooks and maids for the wealthy vacationers. A noted artist, Mayna Avent, purchased a cabin from the Owenby family and used it as a studio for many years.

In 1920 one of the owners of a cottage at Elkmont made a suggestion that would change the area permanently. Willis Davis visited Yellowstone National Park and brought back the idea that the Great Smoky Mountains would be a suitable site for a park. Another cabin owner, David Chapman, supported the concept. In 1925 the Tennessee General Assembly backed the idea, and in 1926 President Calvin Coolidge signed legislation committing the federal government to administer the land as a national park.

Soon 76,000 acres of land were purchased from the Townsend Company. Using the right of "eminent domain," most longtime residents of the area were forced to sell their small holdings, but special treatment was provided for the cabin owners, who received half the value of their property and were given lifetime leases. Around this time the Wonderland Hotel was once again opened to the public.

Following World War II travel became cheaper and more visitors came to the Great Smoky Mountains National Park. The old railroad bed along Little River became a popular hiking trail, as did a path along Jakes Creek, with the Cucumber Gap trail connecting the two, but the hikers using these trails still found themselves passing through a collection of private houses.

In order to get permission for electric lines to be run to the cottages, the association of owners agreed to terminate their leases in 1952. When that date arrived they were reluctant to let go of their summer homes, and an extension of the leases was agreed to, terminating in 1972. They followed the same process in 1972, but faced growing opposition from visitors and conservationists who saw living in Elkmont as a special privilege, reserved for some but not available to all. Public meetings were held, comments were taken from interested parties, and in 1992, most of the leases expired, including that of the Wonderland Park Hotel. The remaining four cabin leases expired in 2001.

The first thought of the National Park Service was to remove all the buildings and allow nature to reclaim the area. However, in 1994, many of the buildings were placed on the National Register of Historic Places, protecting them from being destroyed. Now a new round of debates arose about how to deal with Elkmont, and again public hearings were held to gather ideas. Some proposed that the cabin owners be allowed to pay a fee to the park in order to retain their property. This would produce some revenue for the park and would cost nothing. Others took a very different view, contending that the cabins were a testimony to the influence of wealth, and had no place in a park that was intended to be "a pleasuring-ground free to the people."

Even as a decision was being made, nature took its course. The Wonderland Hotel became so dilapidated by 2005 that the park service decided to carefully document the structure and then tear it down since it had become a safety hazard. The annex to the main hotel building was preserved, but an unexplained fire destroyed that structure in April 2016.

Nothing remains at the site today, and no trails lead to the former location of the Wonderland Park Hotel.

In 2009 the park service decided that while the cabins were old, not all of them were historic, and it was announced that most of them would be torn down. Among the structures to be restored and preserved was the Levi Trentham Cabin, one of the oldest buildings in the park. Another structure chosen for preservation was the cabin that once belonged to the Mayo family. It was chosen because it was a "set off" house—a building used by the timber company to house workers and built to be set on a railcar, moved to a new location, and then set off for occupancy.

Near the Mayo Cabin is a frame structure built around 1920 that was used to house the servants who worked for the summer residents. The Creekmore Cabin was deemed to have historic significance, although a great deal of reconstruction was required to replace rotting walls. The Spence Cabin, dating from 1928, was saved and restored as a space for meetings and small gatherings, while the iconic Appalachian Club building was restored to its original appearance. Both the Spence Cabin and the Appalachian Club can be rented for special occasions, such as family reunions and weddings.

Today Elkmont is hardly a ghost town. It serves as a museum community that interprets the history of the area from its days as a logging camp to a summer resort. What once was called a ghost town has reemerged as a living reminder of the past of the Great Smoky Mountains.

Author's note: The Elkmont "ghost town" is home to one of nature's wonders for about two weeks each year. During the mating season of *Photinus carolinus* in late May to early June, thousands of visitors flock to see these synchronous fireflies. There are nineteen varieties of fireflies, locally called "lightning bugs," but this species flashes in unison. This is probably a part of the mating display and is a competition among the male fireflies. They do not always flash in unison; sometimes the flashes occur in waves, sometimes randomly, but short bursts of synchronous flashing also takes place.

This natural display has become so popular that the park service has found it necessary to set up a lottery to regulate parking at the Sugarlands Visitor Center and to provide shuttle buses from the Visitor Center to Elkmont. More information about the synchronous fireflies can be found on the Great Smoky Mountains National Park website.

2016

Fire on the Mountain

"Fire on the mountain, fire in the air, looks like hell waiting for me there." These are the opening words of an old country song, but they well describe the event that overwhelmed Gatlinburg, Tennessee, on November 28 and 29, 2016. A maelstrom of wind and fire swept down out of the Great Smoky Mountains National Park, engulfing the town which serves as a gateway to the park for many of its ten million annual visitors. This event was both a freak of nature and the probable result of human activity.

Gatlinburg, once known as White Oak Flats, is a community of 3,900 permanent residents that makes available 60,000 hotel, condo, and cabin beds to the visitors who flood into the Great Smoky Mountains National Park. The park surrounds the town on three sides, and there are only

three roads capable of handling the volume of traffic leading into and out of the town. US 441 enters Gatlinburg from
the north, leading from I-75 through Sevierville and Pigeon
Forge before passing through a section of the park to reach
Gatlinburg. This same highway continues south through
the park to Cherokee, North Carolina. Just 2 miles into the
park, US 441 South joins the Little River Road, which runs
through the park westward to Townsend. On the north side
of Gatlinburg, US 441 junctions with US 321 and follows
the park boundary east to Cosby and, eventually, to I-40.
Traffic into and out of the town is often slow because of this
limited road network.

On November 23, 2016, the day before Thanksgiving,
smoke was seen rising in the vicinity of the Chimney Tops
Trail, one of the most popular trails in the park despite its
steep grade leading through challenging topography. Later
it was reported to park rangers that a hiker with a GoPro
camera had filmed two teenagers coming down the trail with
smoke from a fire rising behind them where they had thrown
lighted matches into the dry leaves. The two were later identified by authorities, but because they were juveniles their
names cannot be given. It should be noted that the entire area
was in a condition of severe drought.

A fire had been detected in the Chimney Tops area on
November 13 and given the designation "Chimney Tops
Fire." A containment line was built around this fire, which
burned itself out on November 16, having involved only one-
quarter of an acre. When smoke from the second fire was
spotted in the same general area on November 23, the first
fire had its designation changed to "Chimney Tops 1," and
the newly discovered blaze was named "Chimney Tops 2"
on the day it was spotted.

A very light rain fell on Thanksgiving, just over one-tenth of an inch, and this did not affect the fire. Rangers climbed to the area of the fire and, because of the rugged terrain, decided to let the fire take its course, feeling the fire could be contained to an area of about 410 acres. With this decision, the fire was left alone for the next two days. This was not an unusual decision by the park service; fire is a part of the cycle of nature, and the park service tries not to interfere unnecessarily with that cycle.

Sunday, November 27, saw a change in plans. A Chinook Type 1, the largest helicopter used in fighting fires, began to dump water on the Chimney Tops 2 fire. When this aircraft ran low on fuel, two more Type 1s came to take its place. These helicopters dumped water on the fire for about five hours until darkness forced them to stop. At this time the relative humidity was 17 percent, extremely low for an area where the humidity reaches 80 percent on a regular basis.

The purpose of dumping water on a fire from aircraft is not to extinguish the flames but to slow them down in order to give firefighting crews on the ground a chance to build a firebreak. On Sunday, on-the-ground firefighting crews had not been deployed. Early on Monday morning park maintenance crews reported that the fire was approaching Chimney Tops Picnic Grounds, and firefighting crews were sent to that location to try to save structures there. Humidity was still very low, but the winds were also mild. The weather forecast was worrying some of the park officials. Monday, late in the day, a front was predicted to pass through the area, bringing rain but accompanied by winds up to 30 and 40 miles per hour. Gatlinburg was downhill and downwind of the fire.

The town of Gatlinburg touches the park boundary quite literally. Both commercial and residential areas share property lines with the park. At this point, residents were given a warning that the fire was spreading, and those whose homes were immediately adjacent to the park were advised to evacuate. While there was a pall of smoke drifting into the streets of the town and the smell of smoke was noticeable, no fire was visible, and most residents and visitors went on their way. Significantly, when the fire reached the Chimney Tops Picnic Grounds, US 441 was closed to traffic. As darkness fell park service officials felt apprehension and civil authorities were alerted to the situation, but no emergency had yet been declared. Then the wind began to howl.

The Great Smoky Mountains rise steeply above the topography of the surrounding area and the steep mountain slopes create very strong drafts that may cause strong winds to blow either up or down the sides of the ridges. Although the approaching cold front was predicted to bring winds of 30 to 40 miles per hour, the peculiar terrain of the mountains increased the ferocity of the storm. Gusts of up to 87 miles per hour were recorded in the area of the fire. These winds whirled burning brands aloft and dropped them far downwind, and downhill, of the place where the fire had been burning. Suddenly fires were flaming up in dozens of locations, inside and outside the park boundaries. The Gatlinburg Fire Department was quickly overwhelmed by the extent of the multiple fires. A call for help went out to all fire departments in the area and they responded as quickly as possible, but almost all of them had to approach along US 411 North.

By this time the fire had burned far enough from Chimney Tops toward park headquarters at Sugarlands that the Little River Road was closed. Worse still, fires were spotted between Gatlinburg and Pigeon Forge, threatening the main artery into town from the north. One of the fire units coming to the aid of Gatlinburg was from Sneedville, ninety minutes away. One of the men serving in the Sneedville unit said, "Everywhere you looked

there were fires. It was like driving into hell." Adding to the chaos, the fires and winds were toppling electric power poles, cutting off electricity and starting new fires as the wires shorted out and sparked. The Emergency Management Center lost power and had to depend on backup equipment. Pumping stations delivering water to fire hydrants lost power or, in some cases, burned.

For the people asleep, both residents and visitors, the night became a nightmare.

There are few main roads up the mountainsides where many residences, condos, and cabins are located, so that access to neighborhoods is limited. Because of the terrain some neighborhoods are in "cell-phone shadows," and warnings could not be sent to people sleeping there. As people were awakened by neighbors or emergency workers using loudspeakers on their vehicles, the roads became clogged and traffic crawled. By now fires were springing up along US 321, the only remaining exit from Gatlinburg. Some who made their escape told of driving through walls of flames 15 feet high. Some were not fortunate enough to escape.

Dawn on Tuesday, November 29, brought some relief. Heroic efforts had saved most downtown businesses and had opened limited passage along US 441 North. But the light also revealed human tragedy. Fourteen people had lost their lives, 200 were injured, 150 buildings were destroyed or seriously damaged, 14,000 acres of woodland had been burned, and 10,000 people were without electric power. But the town had survived.

The two young men seen leaving the Chimney Tops area were arrested but were later released. The Judicial District Attorney General felt the wind storm had created a legal "intervening cause" that would lead to their acquittal.

One resident summed up the feelings of most of those living in the area: "There is a sense of devastation and there are memories that were lost, but I think our community has come together and will ultimately be stronger."

BIBLIOGRAPHY

Alderman, Pat. *Nancy Ward/Dragging Canoe*. Johnson City, TN: Overmountain Press, 1978.

Brewer, Alberta and Carson. *Valley So Wild: A Folk History*. Knoxville: East Tennessee Historical Society, 1975.

Brown, Margret Lynn. *The Wild East*. Tallahassee: University Press of Florida, 2000.

Bush, Florence Cope. *Dorie: Woman of the Mountains*. Knoxville: University of Tennessee Press, 1992.

Campbell, Carlos C. *Birth of a National Park in the Great Smoky Mountains*. Knoxville: University of Tennessee Press, 1960.

Crow, Vernon H. *Storm in the Mountains: Thomas' Confederate Legion of Cherokee Indians and Mountaineers*. Cherokee, NC: Press of the Museum of the Cherokee Indian, 1982.

Dunn, Durwood. *Cades Cove: The Life and Death of a Southern Appalachian Community, 1818–1937*. Knoxville: University of Tennessee Press, 1997.

Fishman, Jacob. "Historic Cabins in Elkmont Ghost Town Now Open After Restoration," *Visit My Smokies,* September 28, 2017, www.visitmysmokies.com/blog/pigeon-forge/attractions-pigeon-forge/tips-for-enjoying-one-day-at-dollywood/, accessed March 26, 2018.

Frome, Michael. *Strangers in High Places: The Story of the Great Smoky Mountains*. Garden City, NY: Doubleday & Company, 1966.

Gabbart, Bill. "Looking Back at Fatal Wildfire That Burned into Gatlinburg," *Wildfire Today*, November 22 and 23, 2017, http://wildfiretoday.com/2017/12/19/after-action-review-of-the-chimney-tops-2-fire/, accessed April 26, 2018.

Godbold, E. Stanley, and Mattie U. Russell. *Confederate Colonel and Cherokee Chief: The Life of William Holland Thomas*. Knoxville: University of Tennessee Press, 1990.

Harper, Anna. "The Sad Story of Elkmont, the Hidden Resort Turned Ghost Town in the Smokies," *Roadtripper*, March 26, 2018, https://chronicles.roadtrippers.com/ghost-town-in-the-smokies/, accessed April 14, 2018.

"Hikers Celebrate Margaret Stevenson's 102nd Birthday Atop Mt. LeConte," *Friends of the Smokies*, July 28, 2014, https://friendsofthesmokies.org/blog/hikers-celebrate-margaret-stevenson-102nd-birthday/, accessed June 30, 2018.

Hoig, Stan. *Sequoyah: The Cherokee Genius*. Oklahoma City: Oklahoma Historical Society, 1995.

Hubbard, Ashley. "The Sad History of the Elkmont Ghost Town and Why You Should Visit It Before It's Gone," *A Southern Gypsy*, April 15, 2017, https://asoutherngypsy.com/elkmont-ghost-town/, accessed April 18, 2018.

Jeter, John, Jonah Engel Bromwich, and Niraj Choski. "Gatlinburg Wildfires Force Evacuations: It Was Like Driving Into Hell," *New York Times*, November 29, 2016, www.nytimes.com/2016/11/29/us/gatlinburg-tennessee-wildfire.html, accessed March 25, 2018.

Kephart, Horace. *Our Southern Highlanders*. Knoxville: University of Tennessee Press, 1976. Original Printing, 1913.

Lakin, Matt. "Gatlinburg: Firefighter's Logs Reveal Desperate Tug-of-War with Skyscraper-Sized Flames," *USA Today Network*, August 19, 2017, www.knoxnews.com/story/news/2017/08/13/firefighters-logs-describe-frantic-struggle-against-gatlinburg-wildfire/559091001/, accessed March 29, 2018.

Levinson, Eric, and Tina Burnside. "Charges Dropped Against Youths Accused in Gatlinburg Wildfire," *CNN News*, June 30, 2017, www.cnn.com/2017/06/30/us/gatlinburg-fire-charges-dropped/index.html, accessed May 4, 2018.

Lix, Courtney. "Mayna Avent: Artist in the Woods," *Smokies Life*, Vol. 4, #2, p. 10ff.

———. "Wilma Dykeman: A Voice for the Smokies (and Humankind)," *Smokies Life*, Vol. 9, #2, p. 36ff.

Madden, Robert R., and T. Russell Jones. *Mountain Home: The Walker Family Homestead*. Washington, DC: US Department of the Interior, 1977.

Patterson, Daniel W. *A Tree Accursed, Bobby McMillon and Stories of Frankie Silver*. Chapel Hill: University of North Carolina Press, 2001.

Pierce, Daniel S. *The Great Smokies from Natural Habitat to National Park*. Knoxville: University of Tennessee Press, 2000.

Rozema, Vicki. *Footsteps of the Cherokees: A Guide to the Eastern Homelands of the Cherokee Nation*. Winston-Salem, NC: John F. Blair, 1995.

Schmidt, Ronald, Dwight McCarter, and B. Archer. *Lost! A Ranger's Journal of Search and Rescue*. Yellow Springs, OH: Graphicom Press, 1998.

Shields, A. Randolph. *The Cades Cove Story*. Gatlinburg, TN: Great Smoky Mountains Natural History Association, 1981.

Tumblin, Jim. "Arthur Stupka: Archivist of the Smokies," *Knoxville News-Sentinel*, August 19, 2014.

INDEX

Walker, Louisa, 121, 123
Walker, Margaret, 121, 122, 123
Walker, Mary Elizabeth, 121, 122, 123
Walker, Richard, 77, 78, 79, 80
Walker sisters, 81, 120–24
Ward, Bryant, 17
Ward, Nancy, 17
War of 1812, 25, 142
Washington, DC, 50
Watauga, 14, 17
Watauga Fort, 15
Watauga River, 18
Waynesboro, North Carolina, 54
Wear Cove, 81
Wear Valley, 122
Wednesday Hiking Club, 109
Western Band of the Cherokee, 33
Western Hospital for the Insane, 54
Whaley, Dick, 89

Whaley, Steve, 90
White, Carol, 133
White Oak Flats, Tennessee, 60, 165
Wiggins, Abraham, 42
Wiggins, Margaret, 42
Wilderness Act, 125
Wilderness Society, The, 125
Will-Usdi, 46, 51, 52, 53
Wonderland Club, 160
Wonderland Park Hotel, 160, 162
Woodland Theater, 133, 135
Woodruff, Dorie. *See* Cope, Dorie
World War II, 86, 161
Wurerth, 30

Y

Yellow Flower, 22
Yellowstone National Park, 161
Yonaguska, 45, 46, 47, 48, 49, 51, 52, 53

ABOUT THE AUTHOR

Michael R. Bradley has taught US history at Motlow College in Lynchburg, Tennessee, since 1970. He has hiked and camped in the Great Smoky Mountains National Park for forty-five years. He is now taking his grandson into the park for his first hikes. Bradley is the author of two other Globe Pequot titles, *It Happened in the Revolutionary War* and *It Happened in the Civil War*.